HanMaUm Seon Center

66

Don't just read, practice and apply!
Freedom is found only through
applying and experiencing.

77

Dae Haeng Kun Sunim

The Inner Path of Freedom

The Inner Path of Freedom
First edition, November 15, 1999

Copyright © 1999, HanMaUm Seon Center

ISBN 89-950859-5-9 03220
Canada $ 7.95
U.S. $ 6.95
Korea ₩5,000

The Inner Path of Freedom

The Teachings of Seon Master
Dae Haeng Sunim

HanMaUm Seon Center

Contents

Part 2: Cultivating Mind and Enlightenment

Part 3: Buddhism in Daily Life

Introduction

1. Dae Haeng Sunim[1]

Dae Haeng Sunim was born in 1927 to an aristocratic family of military officers. Their status ensured that the family was originally quite wealthy, but by the time of Sunim's birth their situation was precarious. Imperial Japan's efforts to colonize Korea led to a military occupation of Korea that, beginning in 1905, was progressively more cruel and suffocating. Her father, who had been an officer in the court of the last Korean emperor, continually resisted the Japanese occupation. As a result, when Sunim was six years old, the Japanese military government took her family's house, all their belongings, and their remaining lands, and they were forced to flee with only the clothes they were

---

1) Sunim(스님) is the Korean word for a Buddhist monk or nun. It is also the polite way of addressing a Korean monk or nun.

wearing. The family crossed the Han river and built a dugout hut in the mountains south of Seoul. Their only food was what they could beg or what had been left behind in the fields after the harvest. The relentless tightening of the Japanese stranglehold on Korea, the collapse of the Korean court, and the pitiful situation of their family all filled Sunim's father with dispair and frustration. Although he was always kind and helpful to other people, for some reason he poured out all of his anger and frustration onto Sunim, his eldest daughter. Confused and unable to understand why that was happening, Sunim stayed away from the hut as much as possible. So, although the darkness and strange sounds of the night filled her with fear, Sunim began sleeping in the forest, covering herself with leaves to stay warm.

By the time Sunim was eight years old, those days of hunger and cold had lasted for about two years. She had come a step closer to the principle of nature and the reality of life. Sunim had begun to feel very different. The fear she had felt from being out in the mountains at night had faded, and the dark night had gradually become comfortable, warm, and beautiful. Inside the forest there was no difference between rich and poor, superior and inferior; there was only life. However, the area outside of the forest seemed to be filled with inequality and suffering.

The first thing Sunim wondered about was who formed her, and suddenly one day made her homeless? And why did other people also suffer so much from hunger and diseases? She noticed that none of the trees were the same, and even the rain drops were different, and it seemed so unequal to her. For entire days, she leaned against rocks and thought about this, desperately wanting to know and see the one that made her. Further, as she became older, she was bothered by thoughts that, "If there is no one who formed me, then it would be better to just die!" However, the forest became a source of peace and comfort for her. Although she struggled so much with those kinds of questions, such searching would not have been possible if she hadn't been in the forest.

One day she suddenly knew that her true "Daddy" ("appa" in Korean) was within her. This wasn't the father whom she didn't even dare let see her, but was the "Daddy" that made her, her true owner and the true doer. She cried and cried, calling out "Daddy! Daddy!" filled with joy at knowing that her true "Daddy," her inherent nature, had always been with her.

From that time on, Sunim took what she called "Daddy" as her place of comfort and poured all her love into there. Whenever she silently called "Daddy," she felt as if all rocks, trees, animals and everything became close friends, so close that it seemed as if they were all breathing as one.

She had no desire to obtain something or to get rid of something. With the thought that everything was already known there, she just relied on "Daddy." She just did that naturally and never directed mind outward.

Sunim's father was very stubborn and treated her so harshly that she couldn't endure it. So, she had a firm thought that she would take the Daddy that she felt inside of her as

her father. At that time she did not know about the great
world inside. She just repeatedly called inside to 'Daddy'
because she was only a little girl who was poor and
abandoned. It seemed so surprizing to Sunim, that she who
had nothing was given the infinite taste of the Dharma.

As time went on, Sunim kept insisting, saying, "You
can't be replaced by anything in the entire world. I want to
see you." From inside she felt, "Look in a mirror, I am there."
No matter how many times, or how long she looked in the
mirror, the only thing she saw was her own face. Nothing
else. she was completely baffled. Because she hadn't heard
any Dharma talks or studied any sutras, she didn't understand
the true meaning of that. Sunim was around 18 years old at
that time.

After Korea was liberated in 1945, Sunim wandered
down to Pusan, and there she started a small restaurant for
dock workers and poor people. At the same time, she also
worked as a seamstress, using the fabric from army clothes to
make civilian clothes. Although she was able to feed and
clothe many people, the feeling began to grow within her that
there was a limit to how much she could help people through
material methods. Determined to develop the infinite power
of mind, she followed her inner voice and headed north to the
Odae mountains. In those mountains was the temple of a
great Seon[2] master she had met many years before.

Once there, Sunim became a haengja[3] and entered a

---

2) (禪) Chinese - ch'an, Japanese - zen

meditation hall for Bhikkuni[4] sunims that was near Sangwon temple. After spending three days sitting, she felt like her knees were broken and torn up inside. Suddenly, a thought arose, "What is the reason for destroying the cart like this? Instead, why not pull the cow? What is the foundation that makes these thoughts occur? Who teaches this?" So she left the meditation hall and lived in the forest, studying what the Seon master had told her: "You will die if you sleep deeply for three years while keeping your eyes open." To her there were no such things as keeping precepts or not keeping precepts, shaving off her hair or having long hair; there was only going inward.

In the spring of 1950, Sunim was ordained as a Samini.[5] The Seon master, who was again cutting her hair, asked, "Right now, who is being ordained?"

Sunim answered, "There is no moment of you giving ordination, and there is no moment of me being ordained. A crane just flies over a blue mountain."

The Seon master said, "You should die, then you will see you."

---

3) [haeng-ja] - This is someone who has entered a temple and wants to become a sunim, but who has yet to take formal vows. This is considered a training period usually lasting between one and three years, where the haengja can see if they really want to become a sunim. It also gives the temple a chance to evaluate the prospective sunim.

4) Female sunims who are fully ordained are called Bhikkuni(比丘尼) sunims, while male sunims who are fully ordained are called Bhikku(比丘) sunims. This can also be a polite way of indicating male or female sunims.

5) This is the first level of ordination for a sunim. Women are called Samini(沙彌尼, sramaneri) sunims, and men are called Sami(沙彌, sramanera) sunims. Full ordination usually takes place after at least four more years.

Sunim answered, "Where is the I who should die, and where is the I who should kill?"

He again asked, "Where is your mind?"

Sunim answered, "You must be thirsty. Please have a cup of water."

The Seon master again asked, "If I am a magnet, and you are a nail, then what will happen?"

Sunim answered, "The nail will also become a magnet."

The Seon Master was very pleased and said, "How outstanding! Now, go your own way."

Shortly after this, the Korean War broke out. Before, when Sunim had experienced hardships, it was only she that suffered and so it hadn't really bothered her. But now, seeing the terrible suffering of everyone around her was so painful that it was almost unendurable. At that time, she just lived, without trying to pay attention to her inner nature.

After witnessing the suffering and misery of the war, Sunim again wanted to know more thoroughly the meaning of life. Not content with what she had already understood, she kept asking "What is living? Who am I? Why can't I meet 'Daddy?'" She would continuously practice for days and nights without eating or drinking, but the only answer was "you should die, then you will see you." She gradually realized that she had to completely solve the puzzle of "you should die, then you can see you."

Feeling that it would be alright to give up her physical body if she could meet the self that she had been calling "Daddy," she decided to get rid of her body. She tried several times to kill herself, but each time she failed. Sunim walked without any destination. Her only thought was that she should die at a place where nobody would have to bother with her body. Her feet stopped at the edge of a cliff that overlooked the Han river. But, the moment she looked down at the water, she forgot all about dying. She may have spent half a day standing there, looking at the water. Suddenly she woke up and started walking again. While walking, she thought about the fact that although she had tried several times to destroy her body, she had failed each time. It was then that she understood that breaking up the body is not the way. Tears flowed uncontrollably. At that time, she realized, "Tears are compassion that should become an ocean, and I have to be able to again swallow that ocean." Tears were not tears; instead, they became joy.

Traditionally, Seon practitioners traveled around and visited different Seon masters in order to learn and test their own understanding. However, Dae Haeng Sunim never did that. She never compared herself to anyone else, and was never content to settle for what she had realized. Instead, she just kept going forward while trying to sincerely apply and experiment with what she had realized, without clinging to any experience or understanding.

Sunim spent almost ten more years in the mountains. Always practicing through mind and testing her understanding and experiences, she was completely unconcerned about her body. When she felt that she should eat something, she just ate whatever leaves and grasses were near by. Sometimes she found wild fruit or mushrooms, and once, a farmer gave her some dried beans. Wearing only a light set of summer clothes, she spent the winters under pine trees or in a hole dug in the sand near a river. Her skin was badly cracked and bleeding, her bones could be clearly seen under her skin, and her hair was tied up in a ball using an arrowroot vine. But there were sparks in her eyes.

Although Sunim had many hardships, she has never thought of that practice as asceticism. She was just paying attention to only her true nature. It wasn't that she was trying to do something to her body, she just had no interest in it.

For Sunim, letting go or not letting go did not exist. she only put all of her awareness on the foundation that made her. She did not pay any attention to outside things, she just kept watching only what touched her mind inside. It was like sitting quietly in a grassy field and just watching with a peaceful mind. For a while, even the effort of thinking bothered her, so even if questions arose, she did not struggle with them. While practicing like this, sometimes the solution would suddenly arise and sometimes it would come much later. She spent about a year like this.

Questions such as "What principle is this?" and "Who is doing this?" continuously arose. For example, one day the question arose from inside, "Why is one of your feet bigger than the other?" But when she looked down at her feet they were both the same size! When such questions arose, she thought about them very deeply, without noticing whether it was getting dark or not, or how cold it was. However, she wasn't trying to practice like that, it just happened naturally. Sunim wasn't even aware of her body. Only her mind was clear and bright. Although her eyes were closed, inside it was the same as if she was awake. One time, she spent a few days without moving, and afterwards her whole body was so stiff that she couldn't even move her hands or feet.

One time, when Sunim knelt down to drink from a stream, she saw her reflection in the water. Her face looked very bad, and a thought arose that "Although my mind seems okay, why does my body look like this?" At that moment, a sound from inside came out, "That is also Buddha. Thus inside of that, there is true Buddha. In order for a Buddha to save unenlightened beings, it enters a den of demons or the five types of hells. It can become a frog, a pig, or a dog. So which shape, at which time, can be called Buddha?" This time she clearly saw the nature of her true self, "Daddy," which she had been looking for and calling to for such a long time.

From that moment, Sunim kept going forward from the stage where all things are not two, where self and the foundation of the universe are not different.

By testing what she had experienced so far, Sunim confirmed and strengthened the power of mind. For example, she felt like she could hold the birth and life of the entire universe in one hand. She began to explore the planets, the solar system, the galaxy, and beyond our galaxy. Sunim also paid special attention to diseases, having seen so much suffering caused by them. She would experiment with using the power of mind to cure diseases and later would check to see how the disease had been affected.

Later, while Sunim was in the mountains, she experienced a huge light. She had been sitting in meditation and suddenly felt surrounded by a huge brightness. The light extended in all directions for about four kilometers and filled her with indescribable fulfillment and comfort. Every direction was filled with light, and she saw every single thing in detail. After this experience, she felt like she was always surrounded by this light and that all things and lives were helping her.

Sunim said, "I never raised mind to become a Buddha or to achieve enlightenment. Because I was born into this world, I just wanted to know who I am and what I am. After realizing that my physical body is not me, my consciousness is not me, and my will is not me, I just wanted to know who is my true self and what is my true self after all those other things are gone."

Someone once asked Dae Haeng Sunim what she obtained while practicing in the mountains. Sunim answered, "Most people think there is some concrete stage that is obtained when mind is brightened. However, in fact, nothing to obtain is the principle that is truly obtained. If you say that you have obtained, have reached, have awakened something, then already you have not obtained, not reached, and not awakened. Nothing to obtain, nothing to reach, and nothing to awaken is the principle to obtain, to reach, and to awaken."

Another person asked Sunim whether, in order to

awaken, other people also had to practice in the mountains as she did. Sunim answered, "Of course not. The most important thing is to practice through mind, not the body. I just practiced with whatever confronted me, and those happened to be my circumstances. I was poor and didn't have anyplace to go, so I just practiced like that. Regardless of your circumstances, you have to practice through mind."

By 1961, Dae Haeng Sunim felt that the time was right to settle down. She eventually stopped near Sang-won temple in the Chi-ak mountains. She stayed there in a small hut that was a few hundred meters below the temple. As the word spread that she was staying there, many people came to see her and asked for help with their problems. Sunim spent the next ten years there and in the nearby Wonju area helping whoever she met and gaining many different kinds of experiences.

However, as the years passed, Sunim began to feel that she was not truly helping people. They would come to see her to seek help with whatever problems they faced, but sooner or later another problem would always arise. People needed to know about their own Buddha-nature, their inherent nature, and that their Buddha-nature was the one that could lead them and take care of all their problems.

So, in 1972, Dae Haeng Sunim moved to Anyang City, just south of Seoul, and established the first HanMaUm[6] Seon Center. There she began to teach people about their own true nature and how to rely on that nature. Many people felt attracted to Dae Haeng Sunim's teachings because she showed them how they could practice in everyday life, regardless of how busy they were, what kind of job they had, or what their family situation was like. As time went by, people from more distant areas began asking Dae Haeng Sunim to start a HanMaUm Seon Center in their area. In this way, as of 1999, fourteen branches have been established within Korea, and nine HanMaUm Seon Centers have been established overseas. Dae Haeng Sunim is also the teacher of about 140 sunims, many of whom help maintain the centers and assist people who come to the centers.

Dae Haeng Sunim currently resides at the Anyang HanMaUm Seon Center and meets as many visitors as circumstances permit, usually for an hour or two most mornings. She gives Dharma talks on the first and third Sundays of every month and on special occasions. Additionally, she travels overseas once or twice a year to give Dharma talks.

2. About Dae Haeng Sunim's Dharma Teachings

Everything Dae Haeng Sunim talks about is based upon her own experiences. If she hasn't experienced it for herself, she won't talk about it. Her Dharma Talks are always

---

6) [han-ma-um] - "Han" means one, great, and combined, while "maum" means mind, as well as heart, and also means the universal consciousness that is the same in every thing and every place. Thus "Hanmaum" means the one, great, combined mind, the inter-connectedness of everything, and the wholeness that includes everything.

spontaneous and natural. Depending upon the worries, problems, and level of practice of the audience, her approach may be different, but she always emphasizes that people have, inherent within them, the ability to be completely free. By relying on their foundation, they can dissolve all habits and suffering, deepen their wisdom, and become awakened beings.

Dae Haeng Sunim usually teaches very simply, telling people to believe in their own true self, their Juingong,[7] and to let go of everything that confronts them and entrust it to Juingong. "Believe, let go, and entrust it. And then go forward." According to the circumstances, she also talks in depth about the following related points.

Belief

Everyone has inherent within them the ability to practice and overcome all the things that confront them. Sometimes this has been called Buddha-nature, true self, inherent Buddha, the true doer, etc., but Dae Haeng Sunim uses the term Juingong. We were born with the ability to live as perfectly free people, but because we don't use our minds wisely, we are usually unable to tap into the tremendous resources within us.

---

7) (ju-in-gong) -"Juin" means the true owner, the true doer and "gong" means completely empty, so "Juingong" means the owner, the doer that is empty, that is without any fixed shape, and which always changes and manifests.

Letting go and entrusting

By letting go of and entrusting all the things that confront us to our true nature, Juingong, we stop clinging to things and let our inherent nature take care of everything.

Dae Haeng Sunim tells people that both things that go well and things that don't go well are all being done by Juingong, so everyone should just completely entrust everything to their true nature. "It's the force that has been guiding you over billions of years of evolution up until now, so how can you not believe in it?" Because letting go of likes and dislikes is so hard sometimes, Dae Haeng Sunim compares this practice to the process of dying or killing yourself.

Everything depends upon how you think

Everything follows mind. According to how mind is raised, all material and energy just follow it. Mind does not follow material. It is only because of our fixed ideas about things and our attachments that we can't live freely. All the lives in our body follow our thoughts, so we have to be careful about the courses we set them on. One Thought[8] can be the difference between being in heaven or being in hell.

---

8) One Thought is raising a thought from the foundation, as opposed to the discriminating intellect. One Thought from the foundation will cause all lives in your body to move according to that thought. See Chapter 10, section 2.

Interpret things positively

No matter what it is, because everything depends upon our thoughts, it is important to always view things positively. So Dae Haeng Sunim teaches people to see and interpret everything positively, such as "This happens in order to teach me," "This is my Juingong teaching me," and "That's also how I behaved in the past when I didn't have enough wisdom, so how can I blame them now?" All things that confront you, even dreams, should always be interpreted positively.

The material realm and the non-material realm

Dae Haeng Sunim teaches that everything we can see, feel, hear, taste, touch, and think of is actually only about 50 percent of reality. There is another 50 percent that we usually can't perceive or even imagine. When we try to use just our own knowledge and thoughts, we're using only the material 50 percent. However, when we let go and entrust everything to Juingong, it can use both halves to take care of everything.

See everything as non-dual

Inherently, everything in the universe is non-dual, but because people can usually see only 50 percent, they think that everything exists separately. But Dae Haeng Sunim teaches people to see everything as themselves. One sentence that she wrote for a ceremony says "All beings have the same mind, the same body, the same life, use as one, and eat as one." Another line says "All minds and my mind are not two." Any kind of resentment or anger, regardless of how justified it may seem, will only increase your own suffering.

Daily life itself is Seon

While Dae Haeng Sunim certainly doesn't discourage anyone from practicing sitting meditation, she says that, by itself, it is not Seon. If it is something that you can only do at certain times but not others, then that by itself cannot be Seon. "The Earth doesn't start rotating when you sit down and then stop rotating when you stand up." Seon is moving, standing, sitting, and lying down all put together. Regardless of the names used, true Seon, true cultivation, and true spiritual practice is something that you do 24 hours a day. It is always entrusting everything to Juingong, your inherent nature. You entrust every problem, circumstance, reason, and method; and watch. Then when you have experiences, regardless of small or great, all of this is true Seon.

Experiencing

Dae Haeng Sunim always emphasizes the importance of gaining experiences and trying to experiment with and apply the things we know. It's not enough to just know about something, we have to try to apply it. It is through experiencing truth for ourselves that we can deepen our belief and faith, and develop the courage to let go even more thoroughly.

Practice and enlightenment

Dae Haeng Sunim often tells people that they have to die in order to see their true nature, that is, they have to completely let go of everything, and rely on only Juingong. When this happens, Juingong can come forward. From this point on, true practice begins. At this stage, regardless of what you see, hear, or experience, you have to keep it a secret and let go of it, without talking to people about it or clinging to it. Although this stage may seem very pleasant, you still have to greatly die twice more.[9]

Regardless of where you are in your practice, you always have to let go and return to Juingong all of the things you experience. Let go and return all of the things you know and all of the things you don't know. No matter what kind of experience it may be, you must let go of it. Otherwise, if you cling to those experiences, they will become obstacles to further development.

A note about the current text

The main part of this book has been condensed from

---

9) See Chapter 8, "Enlightenment," section 2, for more about "dying three times."

pages 294-689 of the Korean-language book *Hanmaum Yojon* (Fundamentals of Hanmaum). The editors organized the categories and overall structure, while the text has been taken from various Dharma Talks by Dae Haeng Sunim. Portions of the text have been edited somewhat to fit the various topics.

Hanmaum Yojon was designed to provide a collection of Dae Haeng Sunim's teachings, organized by topic, that could be read from the beginning to the end, or topic by topic. Thus this book follows the same format, but some of the topics have been combined and the number of paragraphs in each section has been reduced.

May all beings benefit from these teachings.

With palms together,
Hanmaum Translation Group
November, 2543 (1999 C.E.)

Part 1
Principles

Chapter 1

Fundamental Questions

1. Who am I?

You should first know your true self well. The questions "Who am I?" and "What am I?" are very important. Although you may think that "I'm just me. What else would I be?" it is not that simple. Where did you come from? If you say that you came from your parents, it means that you were formed by the combination of your parents' sperm and ovum. Are you merely a material, biological combination? No, there is true self, which is not such a material thing. Then where does true self come from? This is the puzzle that we have to solve.

Everything in the world happened after you were born. The world came from you, your family came from you, and every single thing you encounter also came from you. The entire universe happened from the time you were born. What would this world, truth, and teachings be without you? Therefore, you must know your true self, your genuine root and seed. What is it that hears, sees, sits, stands, speaks, and responds clearly at any time and at any place?

It is said that knowing the root of a human being is difficult because it does not have any shape. However, you can't see the root of a tree, but nobody doubts the existence of the root. Can you conclude that your root does not exist, just because it is not visible? A carpenter can build a house as he wants to, but human beings are not like this. You cannot make the kind of child you want to give birth to. No matter what kind of parents you are, you cannot make children like a carpenter makes a house. Then who designed me? Then, really, who am I? We must know the truth of life that is raised by these questions.

2. The Physical Body

The physical body is a kind of shell, but there is something else that moves it. Nevertheless, many people feel that the physical body is truly "me." However, such an "I" is, in fact, merely a burlap sack. When the body becomes worn out, and is ready to be thrown away, what use are the things that you have collected as "mine" during your lifetime.

Observe that your flesh is not eternal, but is fleeting, like clothes you change. Observe that your consciousness is also like this. While observing, you must clearly know that the being called "I" is an insubstantial being, which came out from one place in this world and will disappear at another place. You must also know that this "I" cannot be free from suffering, and that it will be destroyed while suffering. But is this everything? There is true self, the one in charge who takes off old clothes and puts on new clothes.

3. Life and True Self

Would you choose several million dollars? Would you choose world-wide fame? Or, would you choose your life? Because money and fame cannot be more precious than a life, try to be a person who is generous in giving rather than in having. Do not become a small person who takes pleasure from handling gold and precious gems. The infinite and great true treasure is waiting for us right now, within us. The joy of truth is so vast and unlimited that it cannot be compared to anything else in the world. Even world-wide fame is nothing but a dust particle compared to the joy of truth.

When people are born, they have already embraced death as their fate. They are like someone who has received a death sentence that cannot be avoided. However, if you do not think that your life belongs to you, and if you know very clearly that you only manage your life for several decades, then your mind will be peaceful and comfortable, beyond the hindrances of birth and death.

4. What is Buddhism?

The Buddha-dharma illuminates the goal of life and leads us on the way. If we don't know who we are, then we don't know on what basis we should live, or even why to live. The Buddha-dharma shows us who we are and what life is.

Buddhism is not a specific type of teaching. Buddhism is truth itself, not some kind of doctrine. Thus the word "Buddhism" is just a name. If you want to learn Buddhism correctly, then you must know Buddhism as the teaching of truth, not as a religion. Studying Buddhism is to become a Buddha by following the Buddha's teachings. "Buddha" is eternal life, and "-ism"[10] is valuable words of truth.

5. What is Buddha?

Because you exist, Buddha exists. Buddha's shape is your shape, and Buddha's mind is your mind.[11] Buddha-nature is also not something different.

---

10) This definition is based on the Sino-Korean characters for the word "Buddhism" - 佛教.

Buddha is within your mind. Patriarchs, enlightened people, all lives, and Buddha who embraces the universe and encompasses the Three Times;[12] all of these are within your mind. Everyone, even all of your ancestors, are also within your mind. What could you possibly find outside?!

There are Buddhas as much as there are unenlightened beings, and there are unenlightened beings as much as there are Buddhas.

6. What is Buddha-nature?

The Buddha proclaimed, "Because there is Buddha-nature in every life, every life is Buddha." How impressive these words are! The spirit of equality and positiveness taught by the Buddha is so great and extensive that words such as "great" and "noble" are inadequate.

Often people think that they can find Buddha-nature at some new and far away place, after crossing distant rivers and mountains, and experiencing all kinds of hardships; but that is not true. The true treasure is within you. Thus you can

---

11) Mind in this text does not refer to the brain or intellect. Mind has been described as the foundation of everything, and is intangible, invisible, beyond space and time, and has no beginning or end. In Asia, if you ask someone where their mind is, they will point to their chest. It is the character for mind that has been translated as "Heart" in the "Heart Sutra."

12) This means the past, present, and future.

become a Buddha even though you do not know anything. This is why it is said that anyone can become a Buddha. If the true treasure was hidden someplace far away and difficult to get to, then how could it be said that everyone has the same Buddha-nature as the Buddha? The Buddha-dharma is the same everywhere, vast, and unlimited.

Since everything that has life is Buddha, it is said that Buddha-nature is the fundamental place, which encompasses your fundamental life, eternal life, and the whole of this universe. But most people do not know that they are already at the fundamental place. Thus it is not the Buddha who deludes ordinary beings; rather, it is the ordinary beings who delude the Buddha. If you awaken to the Buddha-nature that is within you, then all beings are Buddha, as they are.

Chapter 2

Eternal Truth

1. Hanmaum

Buddha-nature is the great principle that embraces the universe. There is nothing in the universe that does not arise from Buddha-nature. Buddha-nature has existed without beginning, exists now, and will exist forever. Buddha-nature is truth, eternity, and is everything. Buddha-nature is not an individual thing; rather, it is the foundation of every single thing. Buddha-nature is only one, so it is Hanmaum; it is inconceivably large, so it is Hanmaum; and it is the whole, so it is Hanmaum. All things come from it, so it is Hanmaum.

The mind of all lives in the world is one. Among all lives, there is no "you" or "I." Inherently, life is one. Inherently, life is Buddha. Therefore, the inherent mind of life is called Hanmaum. Although each life has it's own individual physical body, inherently, all lives are not two.

The whole universe is directly connected with the fundamental mind of life and the fundamental mind of human beings. The continuous daily life of the world is connected to your foundation. This means the Buddha Realm[13] is connected as one. Since there are no walls and no ceiling, the mind of all Buddhas is your Hanmaum, and the Dharma of all Buddhas is the Dharma of your Hanmaum and your daily life. Like the electricity of one light bulb is identical to that of another light bulb, all things are connected as one to Hanmaum.

2. Juingong (主人空)

Why is it called Juingong? It is the true owner, the true doer, so it is called "Juin(主人)," and it is completely empty, so it is called "gong(空)." Thus it is called Juingong. Your existence is based upon Juingong. What were you before you were born from your parents? A human being is not formed by just the combination of a sperm and ovum, Juingong also

---

13) Buddha Realm(三千大千世界, Literally, "Three thousand, great thousand universe") - "Three" means the past, future and present. "Three" also means the Upper Realm, Middle Realm and Lower Realm. "Thousand" means combining them all together as one. When those are all combined together as one, it can be called "Great thousand universe." This one encompasses everything and functions non-dually. Because this is also what the word "Buddha" means, the "Three thousand, great thousand universe" can also be called the "Buddha Realm."

has to be there. This is like a tree is able to live because of its root. We see the trunk, branches, flowers, and fruit, but nevertheless we know that the tree exists because of the unseen root under the soil, even though we can't see the root. However, you should not think that Juingong is something fixed like the root of a tree. Juingong can be called "Buddha" because it is your foundation and the owner of everything. This is why, in order to know true Buddha, you have to awaken Juingong, which is the foundation of all Buddhas, Bodhisattvas, awakened people, and living beings.

You can call Juingong "Dad" or "Mom." Also, you can call it "the owner of mind," "ordinary mind," "pure water," "life-giving water," or "the pillar of mind." You can call Juingong "one thing" or "inherent nature." You can call Juingong "the thing that does not have anything," or you can call it "Amita Buddha," or "the main Buddha."[14] You can call it "God" or "my love" because it is the fundamental place. Juingong can never be fixed because it can become anything. Juingong is the parents as well as the child, the highest person as well as the lowest person. Juingong is the true self that leads you, no matter what name is used. Juingong is "the I of me" or "the mind of my mind."

To use a tree as a comparison, if I am the fruit, then Juingong is the stem that sustains the fruit. If I am the stem,

14) This usually refers to the central Buddha statue on an altar, but it can also mean our own inherent Buddha.

Juingong is the branch that the stem hangs from. If I am the branch, Juingong is the trunk that the branch comes from. If I am the trunk, then Juingong is the root. The root is the basis of the tree; thus, the trunk, branches, leaves, and fruit all come from it. Like this, all of my thoughts, all of my actions, and all of my true Virtue and Merit come from Juingong. Juingong is my true foundation. My body and thoughts are like branches and leaves which arise and then begin to fade away. Even if the leaves and branches break off and fall away, the root makes new leaves and branches appear. Juingong is also like this.

Juingong was never born and will never die. Although Juingong cannot be seen by physical eyes and cannot be caught by thought, it is the self that is eternal and vast. It has the bright power of great wisdom, and it does not change because it is absolutely pure. Furthermore, it is the self that has unlimited ability. Unenlightened beings exist in different forms, with different names, at different levels, and they are born and die. However, Juingong is also called "Buddha" or "Inherent Buddha" because it is just as it is, even as one becomes ten thousand and ten thousand become one. Therefore, through Juingong, unenlightened beings and Buddha meet, and they are not two.

Juingong doesn't exist someplace else. It is found in the person who is willing to look for it. When we cook, we prepare the ingredients, cook them, and make a delicious meal. Like this, while living as you want and need to, the true nature of Juingong appears in your daily life.

Juingong is a giant furnace. It is the furnace that always exists together with the sincere, invisible, and great saving power[15] of all Buddhas, which always exists together with this visible world. This furnace is inside you. Like metal melts down in a furnace, there is the furnace in which all tears change to compassion and all pain is reborn as feelings of gratitude. Any karma that causes suffering or any kind of disaster is just a snowflake in front of it. Juingong is the mysterious secret of mind, and is the incredible power of Buddha-nature, which every life has. This is the great virtue and power of Juingong.

3. My True Reality

My True Nature

Where did we come from? We came from Juingong, our true self, so we should try to find our true self. True self has always been with us and has always functioned together with us, but we just don't know this. We have to realize that everything comes from true self. The physical body is like buds, leaves, or branches that come out from true self. How

---

15) This is the ability to solve problems and take care of things by raising One Thought. See "One Thought" in the glossary.

can you call the branches or leaves "me," while forgetting about the root? Know the root!

At the point where the "I" that is an unenlightened being is denied, there is something eternal, but it is not the self that is an unenlightened being. It is your true Juingong, the eternal self that was never born, and will never die. It is the self that never gets stained, and is clearly beyond any suffering. It is the self that is precious and blissful beyond comparison, that is never born or disappears, never increases or decreases, and is never dirty or clean. But ordinary people are not able to meet the eternal self because they can't escape from the frame of their own concepts. The eternal self cannot be described by any words or writings, and it cannot be revealed through discussion. Therefore, trying to know it conceptually is like trying to move around inside of a barrel.

From a very long time ago, people raised upside-down, dream-like thoughts. Those became darkness that obscured Hanmaum, which was originally bright and clear. It is like when the bright sun and clear sky cannot be seen because of clouds. People forgot about the sun because they thought that there was no sun, and they forgot the clear sky because it was covered by darkness. Therefore, the place where unenlightened people should return to is the true nature that is inherently Buddha, the sun, and the sky. Your present thoughts and body are just one spot of gray cloud that comes from inherent self. Therefore, it is said that there is no substance to the "I" that people have automatically believed in. However, it is said that there is no substance, not because such reality does not exist, but because which "I," at which moment, could you call your true reality?

Humans, A Combination of the Three

In order for a life to form when parents' sperm and ovum combine, your eternal spark must enter together with them. If the spark of eternal life does not join, you cannot be born, even though the parents' sperm and ovum combine. Therefore, it can be said that the birth of your life is the combination of your mind and life, which have passed through millions of kalpas, with your father's bones and your mother's flesh.

There is a cow, there is a driver, and there is a cart. From the viewpoint of the cart, there is a cow that pulls it. In addition to the cow, there is a driver who holds a compass and controls the cow's direction and movement. Therefore, although the cart is pulled by the cow, there is no moment that the cart moves on its own. From the viewpoint of the cow, although the cow has the ability, it just uses its ability as the driver commands. It can be said that the cow is our potential ability, and the driver is our present consciousness. The driver only raises thoughts. However, this driver thinks that he is both the driver and the cart. Further, the driver does not know that there is a cow that pulls the cart. He knows only 50 percent.

The present world is functioning as the combination of the three: the cow, the driver, and the cart. A wise driver is aware of this fact. From the viewpoint of the driver, he must thoroughly know about both the luggage loaded in the cart and the ability of the cow. Then he can drive the cart well, while controlling the reins and saying, "Whoa! Whoa!" and "Faster! Faster!" He can freely load or unload luggage while on his journey. "Holding the reins" means believing that Juingong does everything, and saying "Whoa! Whoa! Faster! Faster!" means releasing and entrusting everything to Juingong. The whip is the Jujangja.[16] "Loading and unloading luggage" means continuously changing and living daily life. When the driver, who once thought that there was only the cart and himself, knows that he and the cow are not two, then he naturally appreciates the ability of the cow. If you were born as a driver, you must know how to control the cow in order to be a true driver. There is a cow, there is a driver, and there is a cart. They are functioning as the combination of the three.

The Physical Body as a Combination of the Four Elements

Our body is made up of earth, water, fire, and air, which gather and scatter according to karmic affinity.[17] Because the body is only a temporary combination of the four elements, it

---

16) (ju-jang-ja) - This usually refers to the staff carried by Buddhist monks, but it can also mean a person's center of mind.

goes through birth and death time after time. Anything that is subject to birth and death cannot be called true reality. If it is not true reality, which never changes, is never born, and never disappears, then it is merely an illusion. Therefore, it is said that the physical body is a temporary combination as well as an illusion.

If living beings are only a temporary combination, then where is your true self, Juingong? Does it exist separately from this temporary combination? No, it does not. Juingong does not exist separately from what is called the false self. Rather, the foundation of the false self can be called your true self, Juingong. Inherent I, true self, forms your physical body, stays in deep, interacts with the Buddha Realm, and rotates as truth. Then where is your true self? In the arm? In the legs? In the heart? In the brain? It does not exist in any of those places. You cannot find any evidence that true self exists by observing any part of the body. It does not exist in any specific place, but is deep inside. It is so mysterious and profound!

Although the physical body is only a collection of the four elements, there has to be a physical body in order to know the Buddha-dharma. If there is no physical body, nothing can be added or subtracted. Throwing away your body is not the way to know the Buddha-dharma. If you think

17) This is similar to karma, but it refers to the specific connection or attraction between people or things, due to previous karmic relationships.

that the flesh must be thrown away because it is worthless and illusionary, then this is an extremely wrong thought. If there is no physical body, only the spirit remains. Thus you cannot develop, cannot broaden your wisdom, and cannot become a Buddha. Because the son exists, you can know the father, because the servant exists, you can know the owner. You can also know the principle that both the visible and material realms and the invisible and non-material realms function together. If you have no body, then what can you see, hear, feel, and think with? Because there is the tree, you can know the root, and because there is the fruit, you can know the seed. Like this, because there is the physical body, you can know the one life, the one place, Hanmaum Juingong, even though the body is only a temporary, karmic combination of the four elements.

4. The Principle of Non-Duality

Although it is my body, it is not "mine." It is a community. On Earth there are many kinds of animals. Likewise, inside of my body, there are many different kinds of lives. Hence, although it is my body, it is not "mine," or "my body," rather it is a community. Unenlightened people usually think that they own their physical body, but there are several hundred million lives in each of the organs, the heart, liver, stomach, etc. Thus, because of these millions of lives, the organs all function automatically. Therefore, the body is like the container of a small universe. The functioning of the internal organs is the same as that of the universe. All sciences, such as astrophysics, geology, etc., and all philosophies are contained within it.

Our body consists of many layers. In each internal organ, there are billions of cells, and within each of these cells, there are uncountable numbers of microbes. Likewise, even in the intestines there are huge numbers of bacteria. How can you count all of these lives? Like this, the universe consists of uncountable numbers of stars. Among the stars, on one of the planets, Earth, there live uncountable numbers of lives, and one kind are human beings. Even inside of one human being's body there are also numerous different lives. Thus the total number of lives cannot even be imagined. However, if you awaken to the foundation that moves everything, then you will know the functioning of the entire universe and the Dharma-realm,[18] because the foundation and all lives are not separate.

The Buddha's mind and your mind are not two, Buddha's life and your life are not two, and Buddha's body and your body are not two. Also, the life of all things and your life, the mind of all things and your mind, and the body of all things and your body are not two.

---

18) Dharma-realm (法界, dharmadhatu) - All of the material and non-material realms combined together. This also includes the fundamental order and principles according to which the material and non-material realms function.

5. The Principle of Cause and Effect

The net of truth is stretched throughout this universe. It is the net of the Dharma, which is like a fish net or a sieve. It is the net of karmic affinity and the net of the law of karma. Everything we do, everything we say, and everything we think are all caught in this net. This net does not have ears, but it hears every single thing, so it is said that it has "ears that are not ears," or "ears that do not have ears." This net does not have eyes, but it sees every single thing, so it is said that it has "eyes that are not eyes." This mysterious principle, which is often described as a thousand hands and a thousand eyes, is the foundation of the Buddha-dharma.

If you slap another person, sometime later the slap will return to you. If you give a bowl of rice to another person, sometime later a bowl of rice will return to you. Such returning is the iron law. This law is completely thorough. Even though a thought is raised absent-mindedly, it will still absolutely produce effects.

There are people who think, "As long as I can enjoy my life, any means or methods are okay." But you cannot obtain permanent comfort by making just yourself comfortable. Temporary enjoyment cannot solve the fundamental problem. You must know that our life does not end with this present life. Furthermore, you must know the law that everything, even the things that you have done secretly, comes back to you as karma.

Karma that was created in the past has built a house in every corner of the body: in the cells, in the stomach, heart, liver, small intestines, large intestines, kidneys, spine, etc., and works according to its assignment. Bad karma leads toward only evil, and good karma leads toward only goodness. Hence, if the bad outweighs the good, then many serious problems will arise automatically from inside your mind and inside your body. For example, you may be unable to do things as well as you used to, or you may begin to hate others. These then become the causes of worse actions. People usually think that bad actions are things that harm other people. But, in fact, bad actions are also blaming others and not knowing to return everything as something that you have caused, because you see other people as separate from you. What you suffer is the result of your own bad actions.

When you receive and come out with your physical body by borrowing your father's bones and your mother's flesh, you already carry with you the mass of suffering that has been accumulated over billions of kalpas[19] by good karma and bad karma. Because everything is caused by you, there is nothing else that you can blame, such as destiny or fate. According to the level of consciousness of the uncountable

---

19) kalpa (劫) - An immensely long period of time. Traditionally described as the time it would take to wear away a rock that formed a cube ten miles high, wide, and long, if a piece of silk brushed against it once every hundred years.

numbers of lives that are combined as your body, what was input in the past comes out as your present circumstances. No matter whether their level is high or low, these lives have made a tremendous amount of karma. There is no place you can hide to avoid this karma. You will receive, without understanding why, the results of things you have done without knowing. And you will receive, while understanding, the results of those things you have done while knowing. But, if you combine all of these into Juingong, then because you are not separate, all karmic consciousnesses become one cup of water. People say that there are things such as fate or destiny because they don't know this principle.

People try to use their intellect to unravel all of their karma that is completely entangled with uncountable numbers of different causes and effects. It is like trying to melt a frozen lake during the winter by pouring one bucket of hot water onto the ice. It seems to melt a little, but before long the water you poured freezes, so you have only added more ice. Therefore, don't get caught up in worldly things, release them all to mind, and let them melt down automatically. When spring comes, the frozen lake will melt naturally and completely. Returning to the foundation of mind is like welcoming a warm spring after a cold winter.

With One Thought[20] you can melt down all of the evil karma that has accumulated over billions of kalpas. This is because even evil karma is inherently empty. For example, although a cave has been dark for millions of years, the darkness completely disappears the instant a light shines in it. Light can extinguish darkness regardless of how long the darkness has lasted.

6. The Principle of Evolution

Samsara[21] and Rebirth

A person being born and dying is samsara, and growing old after being born is also samsara. The seasons coming one after another is also samsara. Samsara is also a drop of water that feeds and sustains many different lives, while circulating from one to another. Samsara is also the stars being born and disappearing. All things and all lives are living like this. They don't just disappear after living. Instead, they are endlessly rotating. If there was no such cycle of samsara, then how could anyone ever learn about truth?

If mind is functioning only on the basis of the material aspect, it must be reborn again and again, and it must come

---

20) One Thought is raising a thought from the foundation, as opposed to the discriminating intellect. One Thought from the foundation will cause all lives in your body to move according to that thought. See Chapter 10, section 2.
21) samsara (輪廻) - This is the idea that all living things repeatedly pass through life and death. Like a continually spinning wheel, sentient beings are continuously being reborn and dying. In Buddhism, one is said to continually pass through the Three Realms(desire, form and formless) and the six types of existence(god, demi-god, human, animal, hungry ghost, and hell-being).

out as a collection again and again. As long as you see shapes as only shapes, you become an animal, an insect, or a human being. Thus you are called an unenlightened person. If you are caught up in the material, then even though you are reborn, you still fight, steal, or kill, depending upon the habits of your previous lives. If you do not know how to free yourself by cultivating mind, and so enter the road of samsara according to karma and karmic affinity, then this is like falling in deep water without knowing how to swim.

Dying is like taking off clothes, and being born is like putting on clothes that are called a body. It's just like taking off old clothes and putting on new clothes. There's no one who dislikes taking off old clothes and putting on new clothes, but few people like taking off a used body and receiving a new one.

Death is when the unchangeable foundation of mind, Juingong, changes clothes once. When our clothes are worn out, we replace them with new clothes. Like this, Juingong replaces a worn-out body with a new one. Therefore, death is suffering and sorrow only from the viewpoint of used clothes. From the viewpoint of new clothes, death is a joyful birth.

Evolution

Evolution means going forward to a better state. The driving force behind evolution is the function of mind called desire. If there is no desire for evolution, then this world would become tedious and dried out. However, among such desires the last desire is the desire for supreme enlightenment, which is the desire to awaken. Human beings evolve only with such desires. Over the previous millions of kalpas, we have struggled to survive, have chased and been chased, and have gone through many, many terrible times. Now that we have received the body of a human being, how should we raise mind?

Why do we take off our clothes and enter the world of death when the time comes? That is the process of changing our level. Like the process by which a caterpillar becomes a butterfly, or the process by which a larva becomes a cicada, it is the process of forming your body at a higher level. For example, if your legs are short, then you make them longer, or if your legs are long, then you make them shorter by changing shapes. In fact, you continuously do this with complete freedom, as you want to. This process is necessary for human beings because it is the process by which your wisdom flows like spring water and you awaken. When people have learned everything about life through experiences, and become mature, then they naturally become humble. Uncomfortable things or things you wanted to do while alive will all be reflected, as they are, by the shape that you will be reborn with. Now that you have received the body of a human being after passing through millions of kalpas, should you move back down again?

From the perspective of a human being, we may wonder why tiny and seemingly worthless lives exist. But all existence is in the process of evolution. Thus they are our past shapes, our old friends, and the proof of the process of evolving into a human being. The four types of lives[22] have evolved from tiny lives and form a progression from the lowest to the highest. Furthermore, the four types of lives exist inside of every single life's body, and they are evolving inside of each body. Hence, it is very difficult to say which part is the most important or what should be the standard for comparison. Also, it is very difficult to say where the starting point is or where the ending point is. Look at the world, there is no starting point or ending point. Thus it is correct to say that it is the middle path, as it is.

When you look at insects or animals, you must know that they formed an image of that shape and came out like that because that was the most they were capable of imagining. From the perspective of the process of evolution, lives are affected by circumstances and the environment, and adapt themselves to a certain degree. However, the more fundamental things depend upon consciousness. For example, they had a tail, but they felt that it was not needed, so the tail disappeared. When they felt that they needed wings, then wings appeared. There are so many truly mysterious things. Human beings are also like this. If we don't like our present

---

22) The four types of lives are lives born from eggs, born from the womb, born from moisture, and born through transformation.

shape, and if the mind that wants to change is becoming stronger, then the future shape of a human being will change. The shapes of all existence were formed by mind. What is the power that can do this? It is the true mind, Juingong.

Look around at the world; all things that are alive move continuously. Birds and wild animals move quickly, and all worms and tiny lives are also busy with their own lives. All of this is because they want to evolve. Although there are differences in the levels of all lives, they all have mind. Mind is the owner of the body, and mind is like the driver of a car. Thus the body moves only as the mind wants it to. By the way, that mind hopes to have a better today than yesterday, a better tomorrow than today, and works to accomplish this. With such Virtue and Merit[23] of mind, lives are continuously evolving.

The completion of evolution is obtaining great freedom and becoming a Buddha, who has infinite Virtue and Merit. Therefore, all lives are in the process of accomplishing this. Hence, all lives are our brothers and sisters, who are practicing the same as we are. The Three Realms[24] can be said to be a

---

23) Virtue and Merit is helping people or beings unconditionally and non-dually, without any thought of self or other. It becomes Virtue and Merit when you "do without doing," that is, doing something without the thought that "I did..." Because it is done unconditionally, all beings benefit from it.

24) Three Realms (三界, trilokadhatu) - The Three Realms. The Upper Realm, which is the realm of more advanced beings, the Middle Realm, which is the realm of human beings and the Lower Realm, which is the realm of less developed beings and the hell realms.

great school that is full of beings who are practicing the way.

Creation

Evolution and creation are all manifestations of Hanmaum. Evolution means to enhance the level of mind. Once the level of mind changes, the function of the body develops and the shape also changes. Those animals that had huge bodies and looked very ugly in ancient times have disappeared because the level of their mind became bright while they were alive. Creation is exposing the mind's design to the outside. Because there is the mind's design, an evolved body manifests outwardly. Thus, while it is evolution, it is also creation, and while it is creation, it is also evolution.

When an insect that can only crawl wants to fly, even only one time, the mind that wants to fly is the power of evolution. The level of mind moves up, the functions of the body develop, and eventually it takes off its body and can fly as a butterfly. When this happens, such an accomplishment can be called creation. In other words, creation is exposing the mind's design to the outside. However, even if it is created, it does not remain with fixed ideas and fixed behaviors. Thus creation itself is manifestation. Mind is the basis of both evolution and creation, so evolution and creation are not two. De-evolution is also done by mind. All of these are manifestations of mind.

7. The Reality of Truth

Flowing

Truth is the flowing that never stops for even a moment. It flows and penetrates, and is alive. There is nothing in the world that is unmoving; there is only flowing. Without beginning or end, without coming and going, there is only flowing, just as it is. Like flowing water, it flows naturally, without any hindrance. Because it is flowing like water, there is no moment that it ever becomes stagnant. Therefore, stopping something from flowing is the same as killing it.

We live inside of truth. As fish live in water, truth exists in our daily life. If you try to find truth far away, then that is like a fish trying to find something outside of water. Truth does not have time and space, and never stands still for even a second. It is rotating without resting, like people breathe in and breathe out without stopping. It can be called "endlessly circling a pagoda."[25]

The true shape is hidden. No, instead of being inherently hidden, it only appears hidden to unenlightened beings' eyes. The true shape is inherently crystal clear, like something in bright sunlight, but this true shape is not seen by

---

25) "Circling a pagoda" means walking around a pagoda in a circle. Traditionally, this is a devotional practice of showing reverence towards a particular pagoda or stupa.

unenlightened beings. The meaning of "Buddha-dharma" is to correctly see the true shape of all things, it is not something else. When the Buddha taught the Eightfold Noble Path, he first said, "See correctly." If you see correctly, then it is wisdom. If it is wisdom, then it is emancipation. Thus, if unenlightened beings can see correctly, all of the suffering and anguish, irrationality and conflicts that they face will disappear. This is because they will know that those things inherently have no root and are empty, and that the fundamental nature is very clearly eternal.

Manifestation

The world is a giant tree. Its foundation is the root, i.e., Juingong, Buddha itself. The numerous leaves and branches that appear from the root are the phenomenal world. However, it seems like this only because, as a method, we have borrowed words, which explain by dividing. In fact, we have to thoroughly know that everything is one. Each leaf can be compared to a living being, but inherently the root and leaves are not separated.

For example, when waves occur in the sea, many water drops are created. However, if they sink, they all become the water of the sea itself. In this case, water drops can be compared to the shapes of living beings, and the sea can be compared to the fundamental place. A small water drop being created is like a life being born. A small water drop sinking is like a living being taking off its body and returning to the foundation. Like this, at the fundamental place, there is no division between "you" and "me." There is no division between your ancestors and my ancestors. The foundation of life is vast and huge, but it is one. It exists like the calm water of the sea, and from time to time it manifests as large or small. Water drops are created or disappear according to the wind. Like this, the foundation brings out and takes back, and shows the things called birth and death.

If you make a lid for a bowl, then it is a creation. But if you make a lid that can cover anything, at any time, then it is not a creation, it is manifestation.

Emptiness(空) and Nothingness(無)

No single thing is stationary, not even for an instant. Everything just changes and manifests, so there is nothing you can carry with you. Therefore, to the self that has no "self," there is not even suffering. Although there is nothing you can carry with you, you think that you carry some burden, so you bind yourself up with your fixed ideas. If you know that everything changes every instant because it is empty, then you don't attach to or hold onto anything. So, form is empty, thoughts are empty, words are empty, names are empty, everything is empty.

Most people don't know about the non-material realm, so

they tend to cling to the phenomenal world. In order to correct this, it is taught that form is emptiness. But people also easily misunderstand emptiness as a state where there is not a single thing, so they are taught that emptiness is form.

Everything in the Buddha Realm[26] is manifesting right now, so why is it said that everything is empty? Let's look closely at this. Do we have the same unchanging thoughts and perform the same unchanging behaviors for 24 hours a day? Or, instead, do we act like this when meeting this person, and act like that when meeting that person? For 24 hours - without being stationary for even a moment - we speak, think, act, and flow without having to think about it, as a pendulum moves without staying anyplace for even a second. Because everything manifests and changes, you can't say that it is this or that, or whether it exists or not. This is why it is called emptiness.

Emptiness(gong, 空) is not nothingness(mu, 無). It is emptiness that makes existence live, and it is emptiness that is not different from existence. It is emptiness that is continuously creating existence, and it is emptiness that is

---

26) Buddha Realm(三千大千世界, Literally, "Three thousand, great thousand universe") - "Three" means the past, future and present. "Three" also means the Upper Realm, Middle Realm and Lower Realm. "Thousand" means combining them all together as one. When those are all combined together as one, it can be called "Great thousand universe." This one encompasses everything and functions non-dually. Because this is also what the word "Buddha" means, the "Three thousand, great thousand universe" can also be called the "Buddha Realm."

manifesting as existence. While alive, it dies; while dead, it lives. It is called the shape that is flowing and rotating without being stationary for even a moment. Emptiness is not dead emptiness, it is living emptiness. To be empty means to be full. Because it is too diverse to be described by words, Seon masters often just said, "Mu!" Sometimes, even this wasn't enough, so again they said, "Mu!"

Chapter 3

The Realm of Mind

1. Shimsung[27] Science

Even though modern science has advanced so much, it has now begun to reach limitations that it can't overcome. Only by developing mind can we penetrate these limitations. If we do not develop mind, an era will come in which it will be even more difficult to survive. This is because material development and spiritual development must be achieved at the same time. However, because we have emphasized only material development, we are now entering a dead-end road.

From the very beginning, all matter and energy respond according to how human beings raise mind. Without knowing

---

27) Shimsung (심성, 心性) - This is when mind is raised such that the material and non-material realms are combined together and energy and ability come out from them.

this principle, there is a limitation to material science. Thus we have to take a new approach to science by returning to mind. The basis of each individual field of science comes out from mind. So, although many scientists do research in every field, only by knowing mind can we continue to develop.

The speed of light is considered the fastest thing in the universe, but it is not faster than mind. Therefore, if you awaken mind, there is nothing you cannot know and there is no place you cannot reach. Even with the wonderful inventions produced by modern science, you cannot imagine the great power of the Dharma of Buddha. The limitations that modern science faces can be easily overcome if you borrow the mysterious power of mind. For example, for those people who awaken mind, it is not difficult at all to go and look around Mercury, Mars, Jupiter, Venus, etc. Furthermore, they can cure diseases that are considered incurable. They can also freely go and come from not only the four dimensions, but also from the transcendental dimension, which is beyond space and time. I think that the Buddha knew that showing this ability just makes people confused and does not help them, so he was careful about doing such things. If you sincerely believe in the power of mind and awaken, then all issues of ghosts and spirits, which are not visible to physical eyes, can be seen in detail. The principle of mind is the most profound and mysterious of all principles.

2. Shimsung Medicine

Even though medical science has developed so much, strictly speaking, it isn't able to solve much more than 30 percent of the problems. Where can the remaining 70 percent be solved? As long as science deals with only half, even at its best, it cannot possibly solve more than 50 percent. Therefore, in order to fill in the remaining half, we have to develop our ability to use the principle of mind, i.e., Shimsung science, if you want to use the word science. The principle of mind can be applied to become Shimsung medicine, Shimsung physics, Shimsung astronomy, Shimsung engineering, Shimsung geology, Shimsung biology, etc. Unless the subconsciousness and present consciousness combine together and function as one mind, you cannot perform complete research.

If the mind of the ruler of a country is not upright and has no center, and thus is shakable, then not only his ministers and advisors, but also all the people in his country will fall into confusion and be disturbed. If the ruler's mind continues to be shakable, without being centered, then the country will eventually be destroyed. Like this, in your body, if a thought is wrong, then the daily life of the cells that make up your body will be disturbed, and later your body will break down and diseases will occur. Furthermore, if it is confused inside, then enemies will invade from outside. Like this, if you do not center your mind, then outside bacteria or harmful ghosts will trespass, mistakenly thinking that it is a vacant house. Eventually, your body will be ruined.

For example, when you have a disease, if you see the disease as being different from you, then it becomes separate. At that point, the disease can hurt you. However, if you know and believe that you and the foundation of the disease are not two, then the disease cannot hurt you. This is because you never hurt yourself. There is nothing, whether it is disease, poverty, or defilements,[28] that is not you. These are the affairs of Juingong, so entrust them to Juingong. This is true for all other situations. If you do not see any single thing as being separate, accept, and embrace all things as yourself, then all things become you. Hence, the practice that sees every single thing as non-dual gives birth to great power.

3. Shimsung Psychology

When you face difficulties, don't become depressed, saying, "Why do I have such hardships?" When these things happen, you should think, "Now I have the opportunity to grow up." Your future depends upon which way you choose. You already have the power to determine it.

---

28) Defilements(煩惱, klesa) refer to all the properties that dull the mind and are the basis for all unwholesome actions and things that bind people to the cycle of birth and death.

You must know to return all problems to yourself. Think of all suffering and obstacles that confront you as the results of karma that you have made in the past. Do not blame others, do not scorn others, and do not try to shift your burdens onto others. You must know to return everything as something that you have caused and let go to your own emptiness through your own efforts. This is the way you can escape from all suffering, karma, genetics, causes, and effects.

4. Shimsung Astronomy and Alien Life

The unenlightened people on Earth have Earth-type thinking because they are full of thoughts that were created while living on Earth. Earth-type thinking means, for example, that you are caught by the thoughts that you cannot live without air, and that something bad will happen to you if you enter fire or water. Those people who have reached a higher and broader level of consciousness become aware of the existence of a completely different style of life on other planets and worlds.

On a certain planet, all things are done by thought. Eating, wearing, making, and destroying are all done with One Thought. For example, if they want to have a baby, a baby is born by One Thought, without the suffering that might occur if the baby was born through the womb. If it is not wanted, then the baby disappears with One Thought.

They do not need to carry around blood, feces, pus, and urine in the internal organs of the body. Instead, they have an absolutely pure and clean appearance of a human being, and they can taste the Realm of Good Beings.[29] Of course, they are not Buddhas, even though they live in the Realm of Good Beings with such pure shapes.

People rob and are robbed by each other. Like this, the same thing happens among planets, but they do not even know that they have been robbed. If you are ignorant and haven't studied, you cannot even call for help if you are robbed. Hence, you need to improve your ability, then you can try to defend yourself. If you study mind, you can live here as well as there, and you can live as one, ten, a thousand, or ten thousand. Therefore, even if something comes from outside, you can control everything compassionately, such that there is nothing that is not yourself.

People are saying that there is no life on Mars, but you cannot say that people do not live there just because no people are seen. How can they say that there is no life there, when it is so crowded with lives? In this Middle Realm, the Earth, invisible lives are lifted to the upper or sent down to the lower, after being screened and sifted. Like this, each

---

29) Realm of Good Beings(善神世界) - This is traditionally thought of as beings of the Upper Realm who devote their energies to helping human beings and other beings in the Middle and Lower Realms. Dae Haeng Kun Sunim explains this as the workings and manifestation of your mind through the invisible realms.

planet is performing its own assignment. If you do this practice, then because there is the owner of the house, your spirit can never be stolen, your ability can never be stolen, and you will never be experimented on by others. We live in three dimensions, but we can be the object of experiments by those people who live in four dimensions. So far, it has happened that way. Is it okay if it happens like that? In addition, if a competition occurs, the air of ability can be sucked out. At that time, many diseases would occur. However, you would never know who stole it or where they are. If the ability of your genes is completely stolen, then because this is like having all of your blood stolen, only the shell would remain and would turn into dirt and water. However, if the owner is there, no one would dare try to do this. Are you going to live like this?! The reason I'm talking about this is because all people should know this principle, particularly people in the future and people who practice or do research, even if it takes them dozens of lives or billions of years.

Our galaxy is about medium-sized. The galaxy of Tushita Heaven is as huge as 2,970 medium-sized galaxies combined together.

Inside of the galaxy, there is something that bulges like a human breast on each side of the galaxy. Their function is to receive and send signals to every place. The twelve outer stars, which are rotating around the galaxy, are truly brilliant and beautiful. Further, each of the twelve outer stars has twelve outer stars of its own, which are rotating very harmoniously. The shapes of the stars in that area are different from those of the stars here. Their shape is rectangular, and one side looks like the head of the Buddha. Furthermore, if you look at it from above, it looks like a net. If you look at it from the side, it appears to rotate in a circle. And if you look at it from below, it rotates like the bottom of a toy top. It is truly mysterious.

Scientists may say that all phenomena occurred by gathering only earth, water, fire, and air, but without "one life," they cannot occur. When you collect manure in a compost pile, heat and gases are produced, and insects are born. Like this, if winds blow and water and dust gather together, then because things with life combine together, abilities explode. At the moment it happens, there is no good or bad; it just explodes. Those lives that were born like this come to know brightness, and when it is reflected, they become aware of their own condition. This is evolution as well as creation. Without the harmony of Buddha-nature, how can these things be accomplished? When earth, water, fire, and air combine like this, they become the great owner of a castle. This means that earth, water, fire, and air combined, so energy arose and then transformations occurred. Because it changed like this, it can no longer be called just earth, water, fire, and air. In other words, the great owner of a castle was created on the basis of earth, water, fire, and air, i.e., the universe was created. Meanwhile, one day, suddenly One Thought arose, and the universe was divided into three. The middle one is what we usually think of as our universe.

The worms crawling in the dirt think that it is very wide, but they do not realize how big the sky is. Likewise, people live while clinging to Earth-type habits, because they have lived on only Earth. They do not know how to get out of Earth and view it from the perspective of the universe. Further, since they live in this world with a body, they think that they cannot live if the body does not live. They do not know that life continues even though the flesh does not exist. There is no practice that exists apart from mind.

The universe is filled with invisible lives. Not only the Earth, but also other planets are crowded with them. In a body, blood is circulating through arteries and veins, and the internal organs are all doing their own duties. Like this, galaxies and Earth are also continuously moving. Because there are stars inside of stars, they rotate harmoniously. This is because there is the mind that stabilizes them by making them rely on each other.

5. The World after Death

There is no need to ask about what happens after death. The diary called your subconsciousness, in which every single thing you have ever done is carefully recorded, determines what will happen after death.

After you die, karmic consciousnesses cannot tell the difference between a human being and a snake. They cannot distinguish between the body of a bird and the body of a worm. Therefore, if you did many dog-like or viper-like behaviors while you were alive, then you will enter the cave of a dog or a viper. You enter this cave because you think that you see a human couple, and so you are reborn by borrowing their bones and flesh. What can you do about your shape? If you are reborn as an insect or a mole, then you have to live with the body of an insect or a mole. However, you still have the habits that you made while living as a human being, so imagine how suffocated you will feel. This is hell. Meanwhile, while living with that shape, you develop new habits, so when can you escape from that shape? It may take several hundred years or several tens of thousands of years. It is that hard to escape.

Although you took off your body, consciousness remains. But you do not understand that your body does not exist anymore, and you do not know that living people cannot see or hear you. So in some cases, by your own desires, you cause other people to suffer. If this happens, a disease may occur, but no one will know the cause. Or, there may be discord in families or in society, but no one will correctly understand why it happens. If you sincerely cultivate mind while you have a body, then you can leave without having any attachments. Otherwise, if you have attachments to parents, children, etc., then even though you are dead, you will be entangled in all of those attachments. So you will not be able to freely go or return. Instead, you will just wander around as a ghost, and you may be stuck in that state for a very long time.

When people die, if they have never studied mind, then the consciousness itself cannot see and cannot hear, and cannot correctly perceive things in the middle of the darkness, so they often enter the house of a pig or the house of a magpie. However, those people who have studied mind are very bright, so they shine evenly throughout their surroundings. Not only such people, but also their families will live brightly, even though their family doesn't know anything about this principle.

Even though you take off your clothes, your spirit remains untouched. Then, if energy combines with you, you will put on clothes again and be reborn. In order to be reborn like this, there must be energy. This is like the principle with which we can use electricity from power plants. From the viewpoint of this principle, everything is full of energy, so you can become the sun and the sun can become you. While living as Hanmaum, if even stars want to be reborn, this energy must be sufficient. This is regardless of whether their life span is long or short.

Part 2
Cultivating Mind and Enlightenment

Chapter 4

Cultivating Mind[30]

1. What is Mind?

Mind does not have color, shape, location, beginning, or end. Mind cannot be said to be this or that, inside or outside. Mind cannot be divided, cannot be absorbed, and cannot be destroyed. It is beyond time, beyond space, and beyond everything.

Mind is always full, so it can shine like the light of the sun in the middle of empty space. Mind is always complete and as it is, so its ability has no limitation. No one can break it or destroy it. Even if all gods and Buddhas were right here, they could not destroy the foundation of your mind. Although

---

30) This includes learning how mind works, applying that knowledge, experimenting with it, and gaining experiences in order to become a free person. Studying mind, polishing mind, cultivating mind, and practicing mind are all similar expressions.

the sun is very bright and the universe is vast and unlimited, they are not greater than the light of your mind and the ability of your mind.

All things are built on the basis of mind. If mind does not exist, God and Buddha do not exist. If mind does not exist, pleasure, pain, happiness, and sorrow also do not exist. Heaven and hell can exist only after mind exists. People say that God exists, Buddha exists, Heaven exists, or Hell exists. However, these are the results that people's minds create and bring to them. The important point is not whether they exist or not. Rather, it is knowing what binds your mind and then becoming free from it.

2. Cultivating Mind

There is a great treasure inside of mind. The treasure is like a pearl hidden in mud, but it is absolutely there. It is as if you have several million dollars in a bank account, so why do you think that you are poor? Why do you think that you have nothing? The study of Hanmaum is knowing that there is a great treasure within your mind and then finding it. This study is the greatest study in the world. While living freshly with a mind that is open like empty space, you are always overflowing with compassion. What practice could be better than this?

The point of practicing is not to become an "enlightened person." If you know the true taste of the eternal treasure that is inside of your mind, then it does not matter if you are called an awakened person, Kun Sunim, Bodhisattva, or Buddha. People's admiration and respect do not make you happy. Only the springwater of mind, the taste of truth, can quench your thirst. There is nothing in the entire universe that could be traded for the great refuge of mind.

The gains that unenlightened beings are looking for are like being inside of a funnel that gets narrower as you go further in. Thus eventually they destroy their body and push their mind into agony. Others also suffer when this happens. However, the gain that the Buddha-dharma gives is the opposite. It is the road that gets wider as you go further, the road that leads your body and mind to the great brightness of peace and happiness, and it is the road that leads all your neighbors to the bright and warm place.

The biggest issue in our life is whether we step up to a higher dimension, whether we repeat the present dimension, or whether we fall down to a lower dimension. The answer depends upon how you raise your mind. If you awaken true self, then you will see the eternally bright world.

3. The Principle of Mind

All beings live according to the level of their own mind. A child cannot understand the world of adults. Like this, people living on a lower level cannot understand people who live on a higher level, although they are both unenlightened people. Likewise, unenlightened people cannot understand the world of Bodhisattvas.

With mind alone, you can control the universe, you can control the world, and you can control any kind of problem that you may face, such as world peace or the unification of Korea. By helping politicians and scientists to light the lamp of their mind, you can control the problems of a nation and human beings, so that people are greatly benefited and a new future can be developed. With mind, you can solve the problems of the environment and the life span of the Earth, and can control the future of human beings. This is because all things in the Dharma-realm are all Hanmaum.

There are no miracles. All unenlightened beings inherently have omniscient and omnipotent ability. It's just that they don't know this, so they are unable to use it. But there are no miracles apart from this. Do not say that you were given the ability or that a miracle happened, even though diseases were cured or impossible things were accomplished. This is merely a narrow view. There are no miracles. All lives are inherently perfect, so miracles are natural. Rather, it is unusual that you live a life full of limitations. There are no miracles. It is only because most people are not free and are not able to do everything that miracles look special. Flowers blooming and birds singing are also miracles.

The functioning of mind can be compared to a supercomputer. Any thought, once raised, is perfectly recorded. You might believe that a thought is finished because you are no longer aware of it, but that thought did not disappear. Rather, it is perfectly recorded inside of your mind. The thought is stored in the subconsciousness and mobilized to raise thoughts the next time. Therefore, the second thought becomes more willful than the first thought. For example, if the first thought was bad, then the second thought will be a little worse. In this way, it keeps repeating time after time and grows stronger and stronger. Mind is tilted toward the thoughts that often arise. So, if you do not carefully manage all thoughts, then those thoughts gradually grow up and eventually become actions. If mind moves and raises a thought once, it is perfectly recorded. Therefore, the functioning of mind is not limited to just our present consciousness.

Because mind does not have form, there is no place that cannot be reached. It can reach even very deep or very high places, and it can enter even very wide or narrow places. It can penetrate even impregnable silver mountains and iron walls. There is no planet that is too far to reach. Hence, if you know only the principle of mind, then the vast and unlimited ability that can accomplish anything is automatically provided.

In this practice, you teach yourself and you learn from yourself. You let go and you receive. You surrender and you receive the surrender. Like this, polishing mind is the work between you and yourself. Do not talk about the outside, and do not be drawn towards the outside.

There is mind inside of mind. There is fundamental mind which, from the very beginning, is absolutely clean, can never be stained, and is as it is. On the other hand, there is the mind that is the cause of the cycle of life and death. It doesn't know about the existence of the fundamental mind and thinks that ever-changing defilements and delusions are mind. However, although this is true, these minds are not two. Inherently, mind is something that is never created and never disappears. The level of mind changes according to the various thoughts in the present consciousness. Therefore, you have to find mind inside of mind.

However dark storm clouds may be, they cannot stain the sky. Like this, bad minds cannot stain true nature. Even if dark storm clouds are very thick, there is a time when they will disappear. At that time, the sky will be clear and high, as it was before. Even if dark storm clouds pour down rain, the sky is only blocked, remaining clear and blue behind the clouds. Like this, even though darkness is very thick, true mind can never be stained and remains clear and bright.

Chapter 5

Belief

For someone who believes and searches, the day of accomplishment will arrive. Shakyamuni Buddha did not come to receive the respect of unenlightened beings, he came to teach them the way to become a Buddha. Hence, if you have belief, then you will see the absolutely pure nature. Therefore, the first step is important. If you mismatch the first button, then the rest of the buttons will be mismatched. Like this, if someone studies the Buddha-dharma with an unenlightened being's mind, saying, "How could someone like me hope to become a Buddha?" then there are many cases where such people do not know the true taste even after ten or twenty years.

Like a hungry cat stalks a mouse, or a new-born infant cries for milk, if you go forward while holding One Thought of belief as you would hold onto a life-line, then the beginning mind itself is enlightenment.

Those who want to practice should first understand the principles of the foundation and then calm their mind. You must deeply believe that you are already a child of Buddha, that you have already awakened, and that you will eventually reach the sea of the Buddha-dharma, like all water eventually reaches the sea, regardless of the hardships it may have experienced. And you must believe that, when you reach the sea, the numerous sufferings and hardships that you have will melt like snowflakes, and that the eternal world will be displayed before you.

When you sincerely believe and do not step back, you can taste inspiration while solving and experiencing. You understand the meaning, saying, "Ahh! There is also such ability in me!" so you hold firmly, enter, taste, are inspired, and eventually true self appears. When true self appears, and the father and son meet, then together they can freely use the vast and unlimited power that can do anything.

Above all, we have to believe that we have Buddha-nature, the power inside of ourselves with which we can become a Buddha. Then, like a gardener takes care of a flowering plant, we have to make this Buddha-nature live. However, people have forgotten about this Buddha-nature. We know that there is the power inside of plants that causes flowers to bloom and drop according to the season, and then to bloom again in the coming year. But people have forgotten that there is also such Buddha-nature within themselves. This is because, unfortunately, human beings forget all the memories of their previous lives when they change their body. If we can realize that we are at the great moment of evolution after passing through innumerable lives, then we will know that inside of ourselves there is the power with which we can become a Buddha. We will know this in the same way that we know there is the power inside of plants that causes flowers to bloom. We must believe in Buddha-nature, the driving force of evolution.

When a baby learns how to take its first steps, does the baby take a step expecting to walk well or expecting to fall down? The baby just takes steps without thinking about falling down or not. If the baby takes steps like this, then gradually the baby will walk well and even run. Release everything to the fundamental Buddha-nature and go forward. Do this like a baby learning to walk. If you don't believe in your own self, what else can you believe in?

Do you want to believe in empty space or names? Do you want to believe in others' physical appearance? Believe in your inherent nature, believe in your inner father, and believe in your inherent shape. There is no savior better than the savior of mind within yourself. No holy saint or teacher is better than the teacher inside of your mind.

In this present era, in which modern science is advancing so fast, it is difficult for people to spend ten or twenty years before being able to practice mind. So, after considering this problem for a long time, Juingong has been raised up as a road that you can enter immediately. After raising just Juingong, believe in Juingong without any doubts, because all things come out from there and return to there. Questions will naturally arise if you practice like this, so you do not need to receive a hwadu[31] from any Seon teachers. A question comes out from inside yourself, and then you discuss it with yourself. In this way, you can study this quickly in the middle of these rapidly changing times. So even if the Buddha appears here, right now, and gives you a hwadu, do not believe in outer hwadus. The Buddha's mind is combined with the self that keeps watching Juingong, which is bringing in and sending out everything. Firmly believe in Juingong without any doubts, and then you can enter immediately.

Because you do not see true nature, it is difficult to combine with the state before thoughts arise, so let's call your inherent nature "Juingong" and believe. Because you do not yet know, raise your center of mind, Juingong, and go

---

31) Hwadu (話頭, Chin.-hua-tou, Jap.-koan) - Traditionally, the key phrase of an episode from the life of an ancient master(kung-an), which was used for awakening practitioners, and which could not be understood intellectually. This developed into a formal training system using several hundred of the traditional 1,700 kung-ans. But hwadus are also fundamental questions arising from inside that we have to resolve. It has been said that your life itself is the fundamental hwadu that you must first solve.

forward. First, you must believe. Second, you must release everything to that place. Third, you must completely believe that all things you are doing right now are being done by that place. You must do this. In your daily life you should always think as follows: "Juingong! I will never forget that you are my foundation. Juingong! I will never forget that you are doing everything, everything I experience and everything I do. I will never forget that all phenomena are your manifestation."

Chapter 6

The Practice of Watching(觀)[32]

Keep watching. Keep watching your own steps. Keep watching who is talking, who is listening, and who is seeing. Keep observing the fact that all things have been done because you exist. If you are looking for truth outside of daily life, you will never find it. Carefully observe the sense of "me" that cries, laughs, suffers, and is happy. Right there, do the things that you cry and laugh about truly exist? Does the self who cries and laughs truly exist? Keep watching very carefully and closely.

Who did? Who came, who went? Who fell into a mud puddle, and who tries to get out? Who cries and who laughs? Who is the foundation that does this, and who is the foundation that keeps watching this? In your daily life, if you

32) The Korean word that has been translated here as "watching" can also mean observing, being aware, and mindfulness.

continuously search for "who is doing...," you will become aware of the place of emptiness. When that happens, you can keep holding and never lose Juingong. If you hold only Juingong and enter single-mindedly, suddenly true self appears. If you have the mind that never steps back, it's not hard to discover true self.

Watching is letting go as it comes and then continuing to watch. Even if the sky collapses, let go and continue to watch. It is said to let go of everything and watch because everything functions all together. In fact, although you say that you watch all things that confront you, they are all inside of Hanmaum. Thus they do not exist separately. Although this is true, there are still some things that you need to watch, so it is said to let go and watch. If you are doing this, the issue will not be to let go and watch, but will be to watch the self who watches all things that confront you from the inside or the outside.

Even if delusions or fantasies continuously arise when you keep watching, let go of even those thoughts, saying, "They are also Juingong!" Delusive thoughts arise because your belief is weak, but let go of even these and keep watching. You should not see them as being separate. Keep watching all of your behavior, asking, "Who does this?" Letting go is taking all kinds of scraps of metal as they come to you and putting them into the furnace. Watching is continuously observing what comes out of the furnace after you input.

Because you are inherently Buddha, in fact, there is no such thing as practice. If you have strong belief, that is all. If you confidently believe that you are inherently Buddha, that is everything. However, people's innate ability is extremely diverse, so there are many methods. This is the reason there are numerous teachings. But the foundation of all methods is, in fact, to completely return a single thought back inside. So, first I emphasized belief, and then I spoke about letting go of attachments.

Do not overstrain yourself trying to understand this principle. Believe that "My daily life, as it is, is done by the foundation," and let it go. Live while believing and entrusting. Do not try to understand "What is entrusting it to Juingong?" by using your intellect. Just believe that "Things that go well are from there, and things that go badly are also from there. Everything is done by that place, and can be solved by only that place." This is letting go and entrusting it to Juingong. If you always do this in your daily life, you will achieve your great goal. Truly, you will taste the spring water of the universe. However, even before this happens, you will become healthy, your life will become prosperous, your family will become harmonious, and your troubles will disappear. Everything will become better.

Where should you let go to? Let go to emptiness. What is emptiness? Emptiness is the place where all lives are interconnected and functioning together. Then, am I excluded? I am also included there. The whole is empty and I am also empty. Is there anything that can be added to emptiness? Is there anything that can be subtracted from emptiness? The whole is emptiness; thus, inherently, it has already been let go of. But because people do not know this principle, it is said that they should let go to emptiness. In fact, this principle is empty, my body is empty, and everything is empty. It is all empty, such that even what you are doing has no place to stick to. Letting go to emptiness is the only way.

When you release, there are no reasons. You should unconditionally entrust things as soon as they confront you. Entrust things you know and things you do not know, fortune or misfortune, poverty or disease. When you feel that certain things are not going well, you should let go of even these. Let go, saying, "Only Juingong can show me the way." Doing this is the path of emptying your mind; the work of unloading your heavy luggage, which you have carried for hundreds of millions of kalpas; the work of cleaning up the dust of your mind, which has been accumulating for hundreds of millions of kalpas; and is the work of killing yourself.

When you raise thoughts to do something, it is already being done by Juingong. You should not see them as two. You should not think that the commander and the doer exist separately. If you see them as two, then you will go astray. There is only the self that lets go, believes, and entrusts. It is not the self that commands, and it is not the self that doesn't command. If you think that the one who lets go and the one who receives exist separately, then one will become the master and the other a slave.

When you say "Juingong!" and respond "Yes!" who calls and who responds? While responding, you begin to practice completely letting go, believing, and searching. In the beginning, saying "Juingong!" is for letting go completely. Later, it is for believing with a sincere mind. And after you know, it is for going forward freely.

You sleep when you are tired, drink when you are thirsty, and eat when you are hungry. Like this, believe that Juingong takes care of everything, and entrust all things to Juingong. Even a leaf has to fall down sooner or later. However, you cling to your worries, and so cannot go forward. This is why hardships occur. Release and entrust even birth and death to Juingong.

Try to completely rest from all of the things you face right now. Holding and struggling are also attachments. Get out of good or bad, like or dislike, and try to rest completely. Because all karma of the past is loaded at this moment inside of yourself, if you greatly let go of it with One Thought, right now, this is like emptying all of these things. Meanwhile, sometimes you forget to let go and release. When this happens, let go of even this. Your inherent computer gradually unloads the luggage that's been input and becomes lighter, and eventually it will become empty.

Inherently, everybody is naturally going forward while letting go. In fact, there are no such things as holding or letting go. However, people think that something remains or that something really exists. Thus they are caught by such thoughts, so they cannot move as they want and they experience numerous hardships. This is why I say, "Let go, release." Let go and rest such that your mind feels comfortable. Let go again of even this comfort, and finally, let go of even letting go. Then, this is sitting Seon, true Seon, and Seon in daily life.

Because there is nothing to have, there is nothing to throw away. Because there is nothing to throw away, there is nothing to have. Do not go around intentionally loading things into mind. Instead, live while letting go. Let go of everything, without missing any single thing, so that you know that there is not a single thing that you need to obtain or can obtain. Only after knowing this, will you realize that all things are made up of Hanmaum, and that all are harmonious with Hanmaum.

Herd everything such that not a single thing can escape. This is completely letting go of everything. But, if you ignore things, saying, "I was told that everything is already empty...," then you will fall into emptiness and cannot herd.

Thus raise your center of mind, Juingong, at the place where there is neither emptiness nor form. Herd everything to Juingong and enter it. When you are herding like this, your true self will feel suffocated, so it cannot avoid coming out. This is like a new mother squeezing a breast to make milk come out for the first time. This is like leaving only one hole and then herding all of the rabbits towards it. If you herd towards the name Juingong, then because of that name, Juingong will come out.

As you grip a staff that fits your hands very well, grip Juingong.

I want to say to those people who do not yet know Juingong, and whose belief is also weak: In case of emergency, watch by saying, "Because you have done this, you have to solve this!" Believe that only Hanmaum Juingong can prove that you exist now, that spirits exist, and that Buddha-nature exists. Further, while observing, raise mind like this: "Juingong! Only you can solve this. Only you can lead me. Only Juingong can take care of both the things that go well and the things that don't go well."

Releasing to Juingong does not mean that you just sit quietly without doing anything. It is not "I," but Juingong that does everything, whether it is the physiological functioning of your body, or the things you plan and do. Thus just keep watching with your present consciousness and go forward, like a servant who follows the owner. It is like you keep watching yourself while doing, so if your thought of "I am doing..." is not involved, then you will do things without doing.

Even though I say to let go of everything, if a someone attacks you with a knife, just staying there without moving is not letting go.

When you let go of everything completely, the Virtue and Merit of that is infinite. First, all types of hell will collapse. Second, the habits from past lives, which have continued for millions of kalpas according to karmic affinity, will all melt down. Third, the bowl that was full of defilements and delusions will be empty, and eventually there will be nothing to be empty and nothing to be full. Thus true self can be directly discovered. When you discover your true self, the foundation becomes strong. And from then on, you can begin to erect the columns that support the house.

When you let go unconditionally and go forward, the front thought disappears and the thought after that also disappears. Thus you can let go with mindless mind, without the thought of letting go. Only when you are able to do this, will you understand the principle that there is no hindrance anywhere, that you do not block coming things and do not hold leaving things, and the principle of doing without doing.

When you let go of everything and go forward, mindless mind is achieved automatically. If this happens, because you have mindless mind with all things, you can penetrate them all. Thus all directions are completely open, so everything comes in. If you want to use as one, you can use as one. If you want to use as ten thousand, you can use as ten thousand. On the other hand, if you cling to things and do not let go of them, then you cannot move yourself. As a result, you also cannot move the whole.

In order to reach a goal, making a plan and pursuing it is a worldly way. However, the study of mind is different. In true practice, practice itself is the goal and the purpose. Resting mind is not done for the sake of awakening or for the sake of praise or recognition. Because it is just as it is, it is only like that. If you know this and rest deeply, then accomplishment, the goal, and enlightenment will all come naturally.

When people hear "Let go," they often ask, "How can I live if I let go?" However, because you let go, you can truly live. Unenlightened people believe that it is necessary to think carefully about every single thing before actually doing it. However, awakened people never raise thoughts for each thing they do. Instead, they just rest deeply. But still, everything is in accord with the Dharma, without even the slightest error. Because they let go, their actions are more harmonious, natural, profound, sincere, beautiful, and more beneficial than any behaviors that are done by relying on thoughts. Thus it is said that the daily life itself of a true practitioner is the path. This is because moving, staying, sitting, and laying down are all naturally in accord with the Dharma.

Chapter 7

Unceasing Practice

1. The Correct Attitude for Practicing

To a practitioner, tomorrow does not exist. Only here and now exists. You should not postpone things, assuming that the situation will improve tomorrow, and that it will be even better the day after tomorrow. Today, here, right at this moment, you must see directly with an awakening spirit, and must walk like a calm elephant takes steps. "Here and now" is the fundamental place of the Buddha Realm. Today is the day that Buddha comes, and is the place where eternal time is held. Therefore, every moment and every day that the practitioner encounters are eternal and infinite as they are. If you are born into this world today, then you must know, today.

Practitioners are those people who live today as the

eternal today. They are those people who calmly, happily, and silently live every new today. Such people are in a state that is not complete, but they are already complete. They are in the state that has not been reached, but they have already reached it. The true meaning of "the beginning mind itself is enlightenment" exists there. You may sometimes wonder, "When will I finish this long and lengthy practice and become a Buddha?" However, when you rest and let go of even this thought, then you are a true practitioner.

The Buddha taught, "Do not serve me. Instead, take refuge in your own inherent Buddha." However, unenlightened people continuously bow and pray in front of "Holy Buddha." Because they look down upon themselves, they do not believe in the inherent Buddha that is their true self, and just think that "it will be difficult to reach the mysterious and incredible stage of Buddha, even if I practice for millions of kalpas." So instead, they just pray for good fortune. This is not the faith of a brave person. This doesn't mean not to bow respectfully to Buddha. Rather, it means believing that your foundation is also Buddha and having upright independence.

Go forward with the steps that never leave any trace. Accept everything and never refuse anything you face. Do not have the mind that searches for something or does not search for something. Do not have the mind that throws away or does not throw away something. Do not block coming things and do not hold onto leaving things. This is how a truly brave person lives. Become a brave person, who is never stained by or attached to anything. Become a brave person, who is the most common and the most extraordinary. A brave person can run a thousand miles with one step. Although a small-minded person walks for a hundred miles, it doesn't amount to even a single step.

When you throw a net into the sea, fish will be caught, but the water is never caught. Do not become a person who is like a fish. Instead, become a person who is like water.

While trying to make a fire by rubbing two sticks together, if you quit rubbing before any heat is generated, how can you make a fire? The fire comes out from the place that is urgent and determined. Therefore, you must practice without ceasing; don't stop before the fire flares up.

The one who lets go lives, and the one who holds dies. If you let go, you will be a free person. If you cling, you will be a slave. Why do you live as a slave? If you rest deeply, with belief that is as firm as a mountain, then all hardships that you face will be resolved and will go away. Occasionally some cases may be very difficult to solve, and some cases may even become worse. If you are shaken because of this, then you do not yet know the principle of Buddha. When you go forward firmly believing that even those cases are part of the process of practicing, then you can be perfectly free in even those situations.

If you are a true practitioner, there should be no carelessness in the mind that follows truth. You must not be lazy for even a single moment. You must entrust everything and watch.

No matter how trivial a thought may be, you should not ignore it or treat it carelessly, without letting it go. Do not think that you can relax for a long time and then make one great effort. Instead, calmly go forward as consistently as possible. If you go forward like that, without longing for anything, then your mind will naturally open widely and be filled with peace. And the world will become bright and beautiful.

If you understand well the process by which a drop of water reaches the sea after flowing and flowing, then you will not be afraid of stagnating. Instead, you will respond to all coming hardships silently, bravely, and patiently. However, most people can't see beyond the difficulties that confront them right now. This is because they do not have enough wisdom and because their mind wanders around. Peace comes after hardships, and misfortune follows fortune. Fortune and misfortune always come and go like that. Do not look at them separately; instead, see them as a whole. Then, the eye of wisdom becomes bright, and you cannot be caught by fortune or misfortune, hardships or easy times. Wise people sometimes observe from far away, and sometimes they come close and examine in detail.

2. Obstacles to Practicing

The Wall of Fixed Ideas

If there is a prison that is worse than any other prison in the world, it is the prison of thought. If there is any wall in the world that is the most difficult to overcome, it is the wall of fixed ideas. From a certain perspective, practice means escaping from such walls of thought and differences of fixed ideas. Thus, if you think that you are only an unenlightened being, then because of that thought, you cannot play any role other than that of an unenlightened being. Therefore, you should deeply know that a single thought makes a great difference.

There are a lot of people who say that they were born into this world alone and they will die alone. These people do not believe in their true self and the teachings of truth. They do not believe even when I say, "Because mind does not have form, it can explore the entire universe and can function non-dually with everything." These people make a barless prison with their own mind, fall into it, and cannot escape from the sufferings of hell. They refuse to accept that their sufferings are the results of the knots that they have made with their own mind.

Break up all of the fixed ideas that you cling to. Throw away all fixed ideas, such as "I've done something wrong," or "I haven't done anything wrong," etc. These become a wall if you hold onto them.

The Thought of "I"

Clinging to the idea that you and others are different, such that you are unable to even think of "everything is just one," is the fundamental obstacle that blocks the road to Buddha. Attaching to "I" may seem to give you some small benefit, but it is the foundation of evil. It blocks the opportunity to participate in the great benefit of the world of Buddha. Until we know the principle of non-duality, there can be no eternal rest for us. Therefore, as a practitioner, you must not see anything as two, and you must heavily and sincerely let go everything to your own foundation and go forward.

Wisdom is knowing that there is no separate self. Wisdom is knowing that matter and the physical body are merely images in a dream, that they are just water drops created by waves. Ignorance is nothing other than insisting that an individual "I" exits. Ignorance is insisting that "I" exists, while forgetting that the physical body and matter cannot avoid disappearing. If only "I" is thrown away, millions of things will fall asleep.

"My possessions, my thoughts, my fame, what I deserve," all of these imprison you inside of a barrel. Unfortunately, unenlightened people usually think that these are defensive walls that can protect them when they face troubles and difficulties. Therefore, you try to make them higher and thicker as time goes on. However, as you do this, your mind will shrink and become cold. As a result, such a defensive wall is not a wall that protects you, it is a wall that hurts you, a wall that becomes a prison for you.

New things can be put in an empty bowl, but nothing can be put in a bowl that is already full. You cannot put anything into a bowl that is already filled with thoughts of "I," attachments, desires, and the mind of self-pride that insists you are the best. A bowl has to be emptied, then it can benefit from containing new things. When your stomach is empty, you can enjoy food. When your stomach is full, even a sumptuous feast does not taste good. When it has been completely emptied, you can fill it up.

You should be able to find the egotistic pride that is subtly hidden within your mind. Doing this is the work of an honest mind and a wise mind. As you keep polishing your mind, the layers of "me" peel away one by one. Thus the wall between all people and all lives will gradually disappear. The mind that sees everything equally never falls into egotistic pride. Such a mind is on the road that is getting wider and wider.

Because you are empty, "I" does not exist. Nevertheless, people hold onto "I" and wander around for the entire day. Suddenly the sun sets and it becomes evening, so they take off their clothes and go to bed.

Defilements[33] and Delusions

If you do not understand, you should return inward and let go again. However, people have a tendency to fix answers and make decisions with their intellect. You should get rid of such habits. If you really want to study this, you should let go inwardly again and again.

Once, when a centipede was walking, it suddenly saw its shape and thought, "Wait a minute, how can I walk so well without all these legs getting tangled up?" At that instant, the centipede's legs became completely tangled up.

A Seon master once said, "The way of truth is not difficult, the only thing you have to throw away is the mind that discriminates. If you do not have the mind that likes and dislikes, then the way is naturally wide open and is as bright as sunshine." If you want to practice, you have to leave the mind that discriminates and selects. All things are not separate, so what would you discriminate between?

---

33) Defilements(煩惱, klesa) refer to all the properties that dull the mind and are the basis for all unwholesome actions and things that bind people to the cycle of birth and death.

If there were no small trees in this world, big trees could not exist. If there were no crooked trees in this world, straight trees could not exist. This is called harmony. Human beings are also like this. Thus, although you see all things, throw them into the perfectly empty mind and rest. Why do you hold the mind that discriminates between right and wrong, straight and crooked, and thus makes you feel burdened? Throw it away to the perfectly empty place, and go forward with light steps. These are the teachings of the Buddha.

What are 108 defilements? A hundred means nothingness. Eight means four nothingnesses and four existences combined together, so that the world of nothingness and the world of existence interact and rotate together. Like this, those thoughts that interact and rotate together, and arise one after another are called defilements and delusions. These are the whip of practice, with which you can become a Buddha and the Dharma-body.[34] If you awaken, then all defilements, delusions, and desires become wisdom, compassion, and Virtue and Merit.

Lotus flowers bloom inside of mud, and the Buddha-dharma blooms inside of defilements.

---

34) Dharma-body (dharmakaya, 法身) - If One Thought arises, then it is the Dharma-body.

Clinging

You own nothing. Be free from all kinds of possessions. All things belong to the true self, not to the false self. Thus you are merely the manager of various things. Therefore, do possess, but be free from possessing. You must be free from attachments to any ideas of possessing.

If you move your belongings from this room to another room, those belongings are still yours. Like this, inside of your house, there is no discrimination between this room and that room. For those people who never discriminate between "yours" and "mine," there is nothing to possess and nothing to lose. This is because, to such people, possessing merely means moving something from this room to another room. If all rooms are yours, then does it matter if the belongings are in this room or in that room? Perfectly free people use their minds like this. Thus, when necessary, the possession that corresponds to the need is always given. Further, because of this, they are perfectly free people who walk with the entire universe.

Look at the reason you are not free. Is it because of some external authority, expensive clothes, or some other thing? Who is the owner? Is it you, an external authority, fame, or money? Should I exist for the object, or should the object exist for me? Unenlightened people are like slaves who are chained by attachments, greed, and the certificate of slavery.[35]

Don't become attached to your physical body. If you are attached to it, then when you have to leave your body after living your entire life, how can you leave? Thus, at the end of their lives, many people suffer pain for several years. This is like opening a pea pod. If it does not open well, then you have to use a lot of effort. However, if the peas are ripe, the shell comes off easily. Like this, you must not have attachments, then you can freely leave when you want to go.

3. The Practice of True Seon

The Method of Practice

There are numerous methods of practicing. However, if it is not the method of practicing with mind, then when your body falls away, everything else falls away. What will remain to practice with? After mastering this principle, you can practice yoga, contemplation, or sitting meditation as you want. However, you should not do these things just because such names and methods exist.

Flowers bloom automatically when the conditions are appropriate. Nevertheless, people wander around trying to

---

35) This was a document that proved someone was a slave. In Korea, slavery existed up until the mid to late 1800's. All of the slaves were Korean, so the certificate of slavery was the only proof that someone was a slave. As long as it existed they remained a slave, but if it was destroyed, then that person was immediately free.

find something, as if there was some unique and astonishing special method. Instead, they should learn the conditions that cause flowers to bloom, and then create those conditions. First center your mind, and then return those outward thoughts to the inside. Do not be dazzled by or chase after other people's enlightenment. Instead, try to cause the flower of enlightenment that is within you to bloom. Because you are already endowed with it, do not go looking for it, just help it bloom naturally.

If you are provided with a specific method, then in the beginning it may seem visible and graspable. However, as you go further, it will die out and eventually you will hit a wall. However, if you experience the study of letting go and entrusting, then the road that seemed narrow in the beginning will gradually widen. In the end, it will become a great gate.

Some people may feel uncertain or overwhelmed when they first hear about letting go. There are some people who feel that it is very difficult to know what to do when they hear about letting go, because no method or detailed instruction is given. You may feel that you have to use sitting meditation as a method in order to practice. However, your mind does not sit just because your body sits. True Seon is practiced through mind, not through the body. You have to begin by solving problems through mind. If you want to hold your mind by using your body, then this is backwards. From the beginning, do it through mind. This mind should be the mind of true self, not the false self. If your mind goes outward, it is like trying to hold a shadow. Thus it is already wrong, so you can't avoid going astray. This is why we do not use the traditional hwadus to practice.

If your mind feels hurried, nothing will be done well. The middle way is necessary for cultivating mind. Become the practitioner who is very brave but peaceful, and who is gentle but as firm as a diamond. Do not hurry. Instead, believe and let go with the mind that is always consistent, and perform the actions of a Bodhisattva with a peaceful mind. This is true Seon and right practice.

Sitting if you want to sit, standing up if you want to stand, working if you want to work, thinking while you are running, and running while you are thinking: All of these are true Seon. Sitting Seon means that your mind is undisturbed while letting go of everything and believing that all visible and invisible things come out from and return to Juingong. Therefore, sitting meditation is possible at any place and at any time. As long as you let go and entrust with belief, your daily life itself is true Seon.

Hwadu[36)] Seon

Because daily life is a hwadu as well as true Seon, there is no need to receive a hwadu from others or to give a hwadu to others. Your very existence itself is a hwadu. Thus, when you receive a hwadu from someone else, you will not have time to think about true self because you are continuously holding and releasing the hwadu. A hwadu given by someone else is like turning empty millstones or spinning a car's wheels without moving forward. Because people know more as the era evolves, you cannot deal with this rapidly changing world while trying to grip a hwadu. Modern people know so much about science and the world that if they try to practice with hwadus like people in the past did, it can become a big obstacle in developing mind.

Have you ever heard about the Buddha giving a hwadu while he was alive? All directions are naturally wide open, so you enter when you want to enter and you leave when you want to leave. How can you enter or leave if you are gripping a hwadu given by others? When you escape from the barrel, you can roll the barrel. When you escape the body, you can control the body. When you escape the Earth, you can control the Earth. When can you think about yourself if you keep asking, "What is this?"

Because you exist, you are slapped by others. Because you exist, you found Buddhism. Because you exist, the

---

36) Hwadu (話頭, Chin.-hua-tou, Jap.-koan) - Traditionally, the key phrase of an episode from the life of an ancient master(kung-an), which was used for awakening practitioners, and which could not be understood intellectually. This developed into a formal training system using several hundred of the traditional 1,700 kung-ans. But hwadus are also fundamental questions arising from inside that we have to resolve. It has been said that your life itself is the fundamental hwadu that you must first solve.

universe exists. If you did not come into this world, then there would be no suffering, no end of suffering, no path leading to the end of suffering, and this world also would not exist. Because you exist, all things exist. All visible and invisible things arise from yourself and are born from yourself. The time when you came out into this world is the beginning, and your body coming out is a hwadu. Therefore, you must study the principle of emptiness, which is manifesting and rotating, while taking yourself as the foundation and letting go over and over.

What should you do if you want to marry a stone Buddha? Let go of everything to Juingong.

All 1,700 kong-ans[37] arise from Hanmaum, so they will all be solved if you know mind. It is difficult to find the gate because there is no gate. It is difficult to find the gate because there are so many gates. So, where is Hui-ko[38] and where is Bodhidharma?

Naturally Arising Hwadus

Are you going to block the hole that is inherently open, and then ask, "What is it?" What benefit are you going to get by asking, "What is this?" when you know that it is a soda

---

37) This is considered the number of traditional kong-ans (kung-an in Chinese) in the various records of the Seon masters of ancient China.
38) Hui-ko is considered the second patriarch of Chan in China, and was the disciple of the first patriarch, Bodhidharma.

can? Let go of the things you know and move on. Hwadus are merely a method, so if you ask about what you already know, saying, "What is this?" then you will just make yourself confused. If you go forward while letting go, then what you really do not know will arise as questions from the invisible and non-material realm. The seed has already germinated and is growing into a tall tree. Where would you look for the seed that was planted? Where will you go to obtain the ability of the previous seed?

When you leave everything to Juingong, sometimes questions will arise. These questions will suddenly come out from inside, not from the name "Juingong." "Why does it happen like this? It confronts me like this, so why is it said that it is not two? Why is it said that all things are empty? Why is it said that it is not 'me' that does, rather it is true self that does everything?" All kinds of questions will arise. If you go forward while holding only Juingong, then questions will naturally arise. This is true questioning and great questioning. This is questioning that freshly arises, like spring water. Intentionally making questions is like rotating empty millstones. Thus, no feeling arises and only hardships are produced. Intentionally-made questions and naturally arising questions are as different as Heaven and Earth.

Great questioning[39] gives birth to great enlightenment. Great questioning naturally appears from inside after you receive the surrender of all obstacles and after true self appears. These are not made intentionally; rather, they come out naturally. Great questioning is the best questioning, which is given by true self in order to teach you. However, if you go forward while letting go of even that, then you will suddenly awaken, either immediately or sometime later when the time is right.

39) This is sometimes translated as "Great doubt(大疑心)."

Chapter 8

Enlightenment

1. What is Enlightenment?

Enlightenment means never being stained by living and dying, even though you are in the world of creation and disappearance. It is knowing that you do not throw away this world and go to another world. It is knowing that defilements are enlightenment, instead of thinking that you need to cut off defilements in order to reach a new enlightenment. It is knowing that there is no absolute self other than the self that has defilements, delusions, and worries right now. It is knowing that thinking, hearing and false thoughts are all Hanmaum. All of these are enlightenment.

Enlightenment does not mean throwing away the self that is an unenlightened being, and then finding a self that is a Buddha somewhere else. Because you are Buddha, there is no self to throw away, and no self to find. Just get rid of ignorance and delusions, and you will know that you are a Buddha and that you are inherently you. If you become enlightened like this, then you will explode with laughter because of how much effort you spent in order for you to become yourself. However, it is not cynical laughing, it is free and peaceful.

See with inner eyes, not outer eyes. While doing this, the time will come when even the inner eyes disappear. When this happens, you will see with enlightened nature itself. This nature is the universe itself. Therefore, when this happens, all things in the universe are enlightenment as they are. There is no hell, no paradise, no life, and no death there.

If you know only the principle of emptiness and ignore form, or if you ignore present circumstances, saying, "Everything is impermanent," or "There is no self," then this is not the middle way. If you see only one side but not the other side, then you have deviated from the middle way, which is the longitude and latitude of enlightenment.

Take "letting go to Juingong" as the way to practice, and become a perfectly free person. Become a person who sees both the world of visible and material laws, in which unenlightened beings see and live, and the world of higher dimensions, which is not visible to unenlightened beings. Unenlightened people disconnect these two worlds. Thus they suffer and cannot understand why. However, perfectly free people are free from such suffering and can see the world of higher dimensions. Furthermore, not only can they see, they also have the ability to do. This ability to do is, of course, different from the abilities that unenlightened people say they have. Having the ability to do means that, at every moment, you freely and naturally save by becoming one with everything that confronts you.

2. The Inner Path

The Path that isn't a Path

It cannot be said that you have awakened, even if you have found you. Do not make false thoughts like "I am awakened." If you have found yourself, then it is like the sprout that has just come out of the soil. You cannot say that you have awakened, even if the sprout has completely grown and functions harmoniously and non-dually while exchanging mind with all lives and things in the universe. It can be said that you have reached the ultimate stage only when the fruit has ripened and can widely and evenly feed everywhere, and when the seed never stops producing fruit and feeding. Only when the fruit ripens such that it can be given and received by all beings, without ever disappearing, can it be said that you are a perfectly free person who thoroughly knows the Three Times.

In order to achieve enlightenment, you must die three times. Dying the first time means throwing away yourself, and thus obtaining yourself. Dying the second time means throwing away all things, together with yourself, and thus obtaining all things. This is so huge and unlimited that you cannot describe it with words. Dying the third time means throwing away all things, together with yourself, and thus manifesting to all things. This also cannot be described with words. That is why Seon masters transferred this by hitting a table.

While believing in the thing that is before thoughts arise, if you go forward until you awaken it, then this is called seeing your inherent nature. After seeing your inherent nature, if you know and can act according to the principle of great emptiness, in which you and the entire whole function together, then this is called "becoming a Buddha." From there, if you climb the steps that are not steps, thoroughly know that there is nothing to think of as "I," and manifest automatically, then this is called Nirvana. Buddhism teaches us to reach the ultimate stage while alive. You should be reborn while alive.

After you open the door of your mother's womb, and after you open the door of your physical body, you need to open the door of the Earth, and you also need to open the door of the universe. Like this, the number of doors that have no doors is uncountable. Thus you must know the manifestation of the entire universe.

Seeing Your Inherent Nature

This practice can be thought of as having three stages. The first stage, returning the self that is an unenlightened being and letting it go to Juingong, lasts until you know true self. In this stage, a practitioner dies for the first time and is newly born at the same time. In the first stage, a practitioner should make Juingong the center of their mind, collect all the thoughts that are going outward, and entrust all things and obstacles to Juingong. Juingong is your beginning and your end, Juingong is eternal and infinite, so you must return all things to Juingong. Therefore, at this stage, belief is the most important thing. It must be extremely sincere. You also need courage, so that at every moment you can let go of the mind that is caught by various things and circumstances. You need courage because this is killing yourself.

This stage is the practice of breaking up the illusion of the false self, which is made by your own discriminatory thinking. If you can consistently do this, then it can be called true Seon. If the practice of throwing away the false self deepens and becomes extremely genuine, then true nature naturally appears while in the middle of samadhi.[40] It is like the baby being born after the pregnancy. From the viewpoint

---

40) Samadhi has been defined many ways, but it is often described as a non-dualistic state of consciousness in which subject and object become one.

of the self that is an unenlightened being, it is death when this happens, because all things that confront you are entrusted and all attachments are thrown away. However, from the viewpoint of Juingong, it is birth, not death. When true nature appears, you feel indescribable happiness. But this is not the end yet. From this point on, you must live from the perspective of the owner. True practice does not begin until this point.

If your belief is not strong enough, then it is difficult to move forward any further when confusion and problems occur. It is hard to break up the lump of doubt that arises when you watch yourself. And you won't know where you must go or what you must penetrate, because all directions are blocked. When this occurs, people often blame their circumstances or complain about their teacher, and they wander around to this place and that place. When this happens, if you are a true practitioner, you should examine your belief and should not try to find the answer outside. You must die in order to see true self.

Becoming a Buddha

After you know yourself, true practice can begin. In the beginning, you go forward by holding Juingong, and if you find yourself, you will begin to have all kinds of experiences. While living together with all lives, you will begin to practice through all kinds of experiences. This process can be compared to children having toys. They disassemble and reassemble them, and learn everything about them. Then when there is nothing new to be learned from the toys, the children put them aside.

Before you see your inherent nature for the first time, you must practice concentrating into only the one place of the owner. The place of the owner is inherently empty, so it is called a walking stick, a bag, or Juingong. But you can see your inherent nature only when you herd to the one place and eventually let go of even the one. After seeing your inherent nature, you must see and interact with visible unenlightened beings, invisible unenlightened beings, visible lands, and invisible lands. And you must study how to change and manifest with all things at the place where time and space do not exist.

Even if you have found yourself and have become one with your true self, you must continue to practice and go forward from the perspective of knowing true self. This is an extremely difficult period of time. Because you know true self and are not caught by anything, you can reach a very comfortable state after having overcome suffering. Thus it is very easy for you to stay at that stage, saying, "This is it!" Moreover, you will be very happy and comfortable at this stage. It is as if you are drinking the sweet spring water of life, which is not even dreamed of by those people who still wander around inside of suffering. Hence, you will be proud of yourself, and it will be difficult for you to imagine that there are higher dimensions. You cannot even think about higher dimensions because you have never seen or heard about them. However, when you look below, you will see all kinds of people, so it will be easy for you to think that you are the best. Everything above is dark and only below is bright. When this happens, it is very easy to screw up your practice.

If you thoroughly know that all things are your mind, and if you return and release even the subtle powers[41] to your inherent mind, then mindless mind will be achieved. "Mindless mind" does not mean that there is no mind. It is called mindless mind because mind is calm by itself. If this stage of mindless mind deepens, questions such as "Does the self exist or not?" do not arise. At this stage, self is so different from what unenlightened people usually think of as "I," that when they hear about it, they think it means a state where nothing exists at all. But, in fact, you continue living your daily life in the realm of existence. In other words, it is a completely empty state where even mindless mind does not exist. It is a completely empty state, not because there is nothing, but because it is able to be anything. It is the emptiness in which even mindless mind melts, so, as it is, it is the power of dissolving all suffering and ignorance.

---

41) The five subtle powers are the ability to hear anything at any place, the ability to see anything at any place, the ability to know others' thoughts and feelings, the ability to know past, present, and future lives, and the ability to appear anywhere, without moving your body.

Nirvana

You must die one more time after dying twice. In addition, you must keep it a secret. When you reach this stage, although there is clearly "you" and "I," you can become me, and I can become you, without either you or me. In this way, you learn this powerful principle of manifestation. You can do this because mind inherently does not have form, so it can come out as a thousand or ten thousand shapes. Thus it is called tens or hundreds of billions of Transformation-bodies.[42]

If you know this principle, then because you are not caught by causality and samsara, you are free and at ease. Because you are not bound by inner or outer obstacles, you are free. Because you are not fixed as "I," you are free. Sometimes you become a doctor or a nurse, and sometimes a judge, a prosecutor, or a lawyer. Sometimes you become a president, a farmer, or a waitress in a bar. You can do all of this without physically changing. Even though you change several tens of thousands of ways without any limitations, and use and apply all visible and invisible things, there is nothing you are caught by, there is no person or thing you blame, and there is nothing that anyone can accuse you of, so you are called a perfectly free person.

---

42) Transformation-body (化身, nirmanakaya) - When a Dharma-body changes into manifestation-bodies.

After you thoroughly die, the stage of manifestation will open. There are mysterious uses in this stage. The story from the sutra in which the Buddha gathered five hundred parasols and made them into one[43] is not a myth, it is true. It is also true that the parasol shone widely and evenly across the Buddha Realm. When these mysterious uses occur, you are a Buddha if you sit peacefully. You become a Bodhisattva as soon as a thought arises, so you can take care of unenlightened beings and the Three Realms. Thus, such a stage cannot be easily expressed in words. The Buddha-dharma is the mysterious and profound principle with which you can hear in detail all the wishes of unenlightened beings. And you can completely save all unenlightened beings with hands that are not hands. Freeing yourself from birth and death is not the ultimate goal of the Buddha-dharma. It is with the power of the Buddha-dharma that you are always able to do anything, even in the material world. To unenlightened people, there are clearly principles of the material world, but even these principles exist in the palm of Buddha's hand. Nothing in the phenomenal world can occur unless Buddha allows it. Thus it is extremely difficult to understand the great meaning.

While not being caught by anything, you can manifest, respond to, and turn the wheel of fire with absolute freedom. With One Thought, you can melt down the Buddha Realm,

---

43) This story appears in the Vimalakirti-nirdessa Sutra.

and with One Thought you can carry all of the karma in the Buddha Realm. When you can do all this, it is called Nirvana. However, when you let go and throw away even the thought that you have reached Nirvana, then this is complete Nirvana. When you reach complete Nirvana, you will know how to come back to the Nirvana of existence. You must thoroughly experience the place where there is no bone, no flesh, the place where there is nothing.

Part 3
Buddhism in Daily Life

Chapter 9

Buddhism in Daily Life

1. Daily life as the Buddha-dharma

The Buddha-dharma is the fruit that has ten thousand tastes and is the flower that has ten thousand fragrances. It can be said that practitioners are the farmers who raise these fruits, and are the gardeners who tend these flowers. Practicing the Buddha-dharma is the most rewarding and experience-filled kind of gardening, as well as the most fruitful kind of farming. Further, you do not need to disregard all the other things in your daily life in order to do this farming. You can do the farming of the Buddha-dharma while doing your own job. Furthermore, your livelihood is the training material with which you can practice the Buddha-dharma.

Do not look for the Buddha-dharma outside of your daily

life. Never believe that there is something separate from your daily life. All things you experience in your life are the Buddha-dharma. Thus your existence is Buddhism, and your daily life is Buddhism. It is a small task to change your daily life into a Buddhist lifestyle, but it is a great task to deeply awaken to the fact that your daily life and all existence are themselves the Buddha-dharma. Instead of changing your daily life into a Buddhist lifestyle, know that your daily life is truth itself.

If you think Buddhism is merely praying for good fortune, then you cannot be called an educated person who lives in the highly advanced world. Further, you do not have the qualities of a free person. It is wrong to treat Buddhism as a negative and reclusive religion. Buddhism is the teaching of great positiveness and great equality, and that everything is Buddha because Buddha-nature exists within all lives. The current era has changed so much from the past that the true shape of vital and positive Buddhism is more necessary now than at any other time in history.

We were born to practice; we are living in order to practice. Everything you do for 24 hours a day - waking up in the morning, taking a shower, eating meals, working, meeting people, speaking, moving, and sleeping - all such activities must be used for practice. All of these must be used for relying on your true self and for recovering your true self.

From the viewpoint of the Buddha Realm, a human being is as insignificant as a tiny dust particle on the Earth. Nevertheless, this existence, which is like a tiny dust particle, argues about things that are like tiny dust particles, and is not harmonious. Therefore, before you can claim to practice, you must use polite words, be harmonious with others and must not hurt each others' feelings. But everything is over when your body falls away, so when will you be able to know the meaning of life?

If you do not know, then life is the struggle for existence. But if you do know, then life is practice.

2. Everyday Life

Do not insist upon your own fixed ideas. Your stubbornness is your own narrow mind. If mind is wide, then it can embrace the entire world and still not be filled up. However, if mind is narrow, then even a needle cannot enter. So always remain humble and respect everything you encounter, so that you will be able to embrace the entire world. This is taking refuge in the Buddha-dharma, and is the process of becoming a free person. Always lower yourself, so that your mind is always becoming humble. Be humble. If you are generous, then the fragrance of your mind will melt other's minds.

In Buddhism, there are three things that are said to be very difficult. It is difficult to be born as a human being, it is more difficult to meet the Buddha-dharma, and it is the most difficult to practice and obtain enlightenment. However, on the other hand, it is said that "begun is half done." Because we were born as human beings, you can see that we are each half way to becoming a Buddha. Meanwhile, at this very fortunate point, think about who makes you stand here. We must have a thankful mind towards our parents and ancestors. This is the reason people bow their heads in front of the memorial for their ancestors. However, let's think about this. Is there a better way to show them respect? Yes, there is. The best way to show respect for them is for you to truly practice. There are good sons and daughters who revere the bodies, and there are good sons and daughters who revere the deep meaning.

No matter how great they sound or how much sense they make, those words that do not contain truth are like fried seeds. Thus, even though they are planted in good soil, they cannot open and produce sprouts. If you are a practitioner, your words should not be only words. Once you open your mouth and speak about the Dharma, then there must be Virtue and Merit, not only for the listeners, but also for yourself. Become a true practitioner who speaks like this.

Unenlightened lives come out from inside of Buddha, and Buddha comes out from inside of unenlightened lives.

Thus all of these are Hanmaum. Do not blame others, and do not be greedy for others' possessions. While throwing away your egotistic thoughts and always being humble, raise mind for others, teach them about the Dharma, and speak compassionately to them. No matter whether it is with words or mind, always treat others with compassion and benevolence. All beings are always interdependent, each one depends upon the others. For example, in a company, there must be a president in order for there to be employees, and there must be employees in order for there to be a president. Therefore, when each person cares for each other and lives generously and open-mindedly, everyone will naturally be taken care of.

If you truly love others, then treat them with compassion. Letting them go free is also love and compassion.

When others seem worthless, ugly, or hateful, you should know that you also looked just like that when you were ignorant and didn't know any better. And you should be able to give love and compassion with generosity and wisdom. You have had numerous shapes as you have lived over millions of kalpas, so how can you throw away other beings, saying, "Not you," because they can't do things well or because they do bad things.

With speechless sorrow, a mother embraces her child who has stolen. Like this, embrace other people's actions with mind and raise the mind of compassion. Do not make karma with your body, mouth, or thoughts by trying to distinguish whether what they did was wrong or right. Instead, try to raise an all-encompassing mind.

3. Daily Life in Society

If water flows into a lake and cannot flow out, then it will certainly become stagnant. In other words, once you eat, you must release it in order to live. All possessions are like this. Think of all property as flowing water. Although it is in front of you right now, before long, it will flow away. And it must flow, so let it flow. Do not try to block the flowing. Possessions are also endlessly flowing according to the principle of this universe, which never stops for even a moment. After flowing out, new things flow in. If water doesn't flow, then it will become stagnant and give off a bad smell, and will eventually dry up. Mind is also like this. Thus, if you do not give and receive with each other, and do not help each other, then algae will appear, and your mind will become rotten and give off bad smells.

Even though you happen to have a lot of money, at some time in the future that money will leave, so think that you manage it, instead of owning it. It is not your money, it is also not others' money. Rather, it is the money that keeps circulating. Thus release the mind of attachment into the bottomless hole. I'm not saying that you should not possess money, or that you should not love. Rather, know your own means and live within them. Do not cling to things; instead, live harmoniously by knowing that there is nothing that is not you.

You dislike others when they do something that you think is wrong, and you like them when they do something well. This is true even between married couples and between parents and children. Further, you feel good when others say nice things to you, and you feel bad when they sincerely point out your mistakes. If you feel good about something, you like it. But if you don't like it, you may become angry. All of these harm you, so let go of all of them to Juingong, and always face things with a smile and good words. If you do this, then true self, inherent Buddha, controls all minds through wireless communications and makes them harmonious. This is possible because of your true belief.

If your spouse or children do bad things, never react to them with your mouth, body, or material things. Just entrust everything to mind and observe. Just let go of everything to mind. Then you can communicate with each other. If you dial the telephone from your side, the phone will ring on the other side. When you do this, your sincere mind will be transmitted. This is truly loving, and is the Buddha-dharma of this era.

One subconscious thought can ruin your life, or it can save your life. Wealth, harmony, wisdom, and health, all depend upon the difference of a subconscious thought. For example, parents' behavior is automatically input into their children's brain, where it determines the child's future.

If you feel bad, become angry, blame, cry, or laugh about everything you see, hear, and experience during daily life, then there is nothing you can become other than a worn-out sack. If you blame the era, the nation, resent your parents, and are unhappy with your neighbors, then through your own behavior, you will become a ragged, useless sack.

The Buddha's Pure Land is not something that exists separately. If you cultivate mind, Buddha's Pure Land will be achieved automatically. For example, if all people cared about the life of an insect as much as they care about their own life, disorders and evil things would not occur. Because you are inherently empty, if you just throw away "me," then disturbances and crimes cannot exist.

From their viewpoint, human beings consider nature as something to destroy or to build upon. In most cases, people raise thoughts like "I am doing..." when they do such things. Thus the result becomes bad karma and will eventually come back to them. Therefore, they must develop it for good purposes, without raising thoughts of "I." Only then will both nature and human beings be able to live in harmony.

The reason big disasters occur in this world, why many people die of hunger, die in wars, and die in volcanic eruptions, is because fighting occurs in the invisible world of mind.

Chapter 10

Putting Buddhism into Practice

1. Applying Buddhism

Even if Shakyamuni Buddha is right in front of you, you must know yourself first. Do not rely on his physical body. Instead, follow his teachings and enlighten your own mind. The Buddha only shows the way, so you must fill your stomach through your own efforts. All actions and behaviors come out from and return to your mind, so why do you keep asking the Buddha to make you enlightened? That truthful mind itself, with which all Seon masters have taught the principle of mind, is the path and Buddha. There is nothing else that can be called the path. If they had tried to teach by showing something with their own physical body, then it would have been just magic tricks that deceived people. In this case, it's as if they are eating instead of you. But you must be able to find and eat your own food, then your stomach can be full.

If you are truly moved by the greatness of the Buddha, then you should do as he did. If you think that the way the Patriarchs practiced was so noble, because they practiced so hard that they never cared about what happened to their bodies, then you must follow their example. In other words, you should not just be a Buddhist who just feels good, who is truthful and beautiful only in their thoughts. The Buddha and Seon masters did not understand the truth, they experienced the truth!

Even if you memorize the entire Tripitaka,[44] even if you completely master the theoretical foundations of all the sutras, and even if you remember many beautiful metaphors and phrases, you will not be better than the person who puts these teachings into practice only one time. When you are thirsty, you must be able to take a drink of water, instead of just knowing what kind of water is good for your health, or what kind of cup is good to drink from.

After the sun sets in the west, where did the children who were playing go?

Try to experience the power of true self, even in tiny things. This means that you should not rely on the

---

44) The canon of Buddhist scriptures.

discriminating mind, other powers, or various methods for those difficulties that you face in your daily life. Instead, try to rely on the infinite ability of the power plant that exists within you. By doing this, little by little, you can feel the inner power that comes from mind. The principle of mind can be known only through experiences, by those people who have experienced. It cannot be known through words.

No matter whether you have ten employees or a hundred employees, they are useless if you do not use them. Like this, although there is infinite ability within your foundation, it is useless if you do not use it. If you believe in the ability and use it, then you become a Buddha. On the other hand, if you cannot use the ability because you do not believe in it, then you are an unenlightened being. Why is the great and unlimited Dharma of Buddha used narrowly and unwisely, instead of being used widely and wisely? Why do people confuse the teachings of the Buddha with superstition? If you know this principle, then through even the pores of your skin, you can use tens of thousands of Buddhas and Bodhisattvas as protective spirits or as Transformation-bodies. Further, you can use even a dead leaf that is blowing around on the ground as a protective spirit.

2. One Thought

"One Thought" means raising a thought from the

foundation, which exists before any thoughts arise. By raising thoughts, you can manage things in the material realm and non-material realm, from the trivial to the significant, with mindless mind. When you can do this, your thoughts themselves become Dharma.

While letting go of everything to the foundation, if you keep going forward, everything becomes the same mind, Hanmaum. Then if you raise a thought, it becomes One Thought. Ordinarily your thoughts are just thoughts. However, the thought of an enlightened being, a Buddha, is One Thought. One Thought! It is One Thought because the consciousnesses of all lives are combined together as one with the mind of that Buddha. It means that they have combined all consciousnesses as one and received their surrender. Thus the minds of Buddhas are also the minds of Bodhisattvas.

Letting go to Juingong and resting means returning to your inherent place. Because all things, visible and invisible, come from that one place, if you return to that place and raise One Thought, then that thought will automatically become Dharma. One Thought at that moment is like pushing a button that starts everything operating automatically. All things will be done as you have raised thoughts. This is because all things are the very thoughts that have been raised from the foundation. When you let go of everything, then with One Thought you can go a thousand miles, you can go to the world of the dead in an instant, you can go to the future, and you can go to the past.

Because all lives, even small insects, are connected with one wire, if you hold the center of your mind, then with One Thought it is possible to send and receive signals, regardless of what kind of problem it may be. For example, if the thought arises that the wind should not blow any longer, then without words and without feet, it is sent and everything instantly receives it. Sending and receiving signals is possible not only with those things that occur within your body, but also with any kind of problems among living beings or in the Dharma-realm. Therefore, if you raise mind as a separate, individual being, then it will be powerless. However, if you raise mind from the self that is the collection of all beings, then it will be vast and unlimited, and it will never disappear. Thus, when mind is raised, it automatically becomes Dharma.

If you mistakenly raise One Thought, then 84,000 defilements enter and leave through a single pore. If you raise One Thought well, then 84,000 Buddhas enter and leave. If no thoughts arise and it stands still, then it can be called Buddha or the empty place. However, if One Thought arises, then all things enter and leave. So, if you raise bad thoughts, it will change and become hell. If you raise good thoughts, it will change and become paradise. With One Thought, you move up to the Upper Realms or down to the Lower Realms.

When you have a bad thought, the consciousnesses inside of you function as one according to the bad thought. And when you have a good thought, those consciousnesses function as one according to the good thought. Why is that? It is because those consciousnesses do not possess freedom and unrestricted power. Because they are not free, they can only move as you think. That is why I always say, "Raise a good thought! Have good thoughts!" Don't blame others. Don't hate others. Regard others' bodies as your own. Regard others' pain as yours. When you see a person who is doing bad, know that, "During the countless kalpas that I have passed through, there is no shape that I did not have. Because it is certain that I have been every kind of life, that shape was also once my shape." Know that you and that person are non-dual.

If mind is sincere, kind, and upright, then no matter whether you know the Buddha-dharma or not, and although you may not pray and bow thousands of times, One Thought becomes Dharma. However, if mind is not completely sincere, then action is also not completely sincere.

Raise thoughts from the place that does not stand still. If you raise thoughts from a place that stands still, then you will be caught by outside things and will be a slave to the world of existence. On the other hand, if you ignore outside things, then you have already raised thoughts from a place that stands still. Thus you will become a slave to the world of non-existence. If you sincerely believe in your eternal friend, your Buddha-nature, then you will know the place where thoughts arise.

If you can make all of the lives inside your body surrender, then all those consciousnesses will be transformed into Bodhisattvas. Those Bodhisattvas also will change into tens of billions of Transformation-bodies. If you raise One Thought, all those consciousnesses can change. For example, they can change into elemental particles, move, and then form whatever substance is needed or do whatever is necessary. Like this, they can control everything. Thus this means that all unenlightened beings can be saved.

3. The Principle of Using

The way of using does not exist separately. "Using" does not mean some fixed method. If compared to a bowl, then it is a completely empty bowl. You can go forward naturally from the place that is beyond words, and where the thoughts "you" and "I" are not raised. But this does not mean that you shouldn't think. If you don't raise mind, then you are a corpse. Raising mind is developing. When everything has been let go of to the fundamental mind, your actions are naturally "using" as they are. Using means that you let go and do while taking care of everything in your daily life. If the bowl is empty, it is using as it is and it is true Seon as it is, regardless of whether you call it "Juingong" or not. If One Thought arises from the place where even the words "the bowl is empty" do not arise, then because the whole functions together, it is automatically using the mysterious and profound Dharma.

Although it is said that eating, sleeping, and working are all the functioning of mind as they are, if you hear this and carelessly think that "everything is the functioning of mind," then you will not be able to see the state before thoughts arise. If you know the principle, then everything is the functioning of mind, as it is. However, in the beginning, because you don't know this for yourself, you have to herd all the things called "functions of mind" into one place. And then you must deeply search for who does this, for where uses come out from, for where words come out from, and for where thoughts arise from. Believe, let go, and entrust.

Inside the path there are subtle abilities. Truly mysterious uses come out from the state that is completely empty, where everything constantly changes from moment to moment, and where there is nothing to raise up. However, you should not be caught by subtle powers. It is said that "the five subtle powers are not the way" because, although it is the same subtle power, it is mysterious uses if it comes out from the empty place. But it is a wrong path if it comes out for the sake of subtle power itself. The foundation is completely empty and quiet.

Mysterious use of the five subtle powers is like using electricity by plugging a cord into an outlet. Although the electricity is the same, the uses are diverse. By the way, such electricity of nothingness is always abundant and overflowing in the empty space. Only those people who believe in it can use it. Only those people who open their eyes can use it. When you completely operate the power plant of your mind, lights come on and shine brightly upon both you and others. In fact, the power plant has already been built and any unenlightened being can use it, but most people just don't know how to turn it on. Further, it is inherently shining, they just don't know it. Without the process of letting go, you cannot obtain such a precious treasure.

4. Pregnancy and Children

Before getting pregnant, you need to be prepared to educate the fetus.[45] When we erect a column, we have to clean and level the ground first, in order to make a firm foundation. Like this, we need to prepare for the fetus even before getting pregnant. We should always try to make our mind tidy and clean before getting pregnant.

How well someone is prepared to educate the fetus is an important factor in the determination of where a particular

---

45) Here "fetus" means the unborn child from the time of conception to birth.

spirit is sent. If you entrust and watch very sincerely, then you will be able to receive a good spirit. Because your mind is so sincere, you will receive a spirit with a higher level of mind.

Whether you have a great child or not, and whether you have a healthy child or not, all depend upon the education of the fetus. All of these things depend upon your thoughts.

The education of the fetus depends upon how you use your mind. First, release and entrust everything to Juingong. Next, raise mind for the fetus. When you educate the fetus like this, you entrust to Juingong all things such as the fetus having a good shape, a good personality, and a mind filled with wisdom. If you do this over and over, then, as Hanmaum, you can communicate all those things to your fetus.

During the pregnancy, if you can educate the fetus well, then it will listen to you and will practice according to what you teach. Although your fetus may have problems caused by genetics, karma, cause and effect, micro-organisms or spirits, you can educate the fetus such that all of those problems disappear. Thus it can come out into this world with clean and clear mind. If you educate your fetus, then any problems that the fetus may have will disappear one after another. This is why the education of the fetus is so important.

Karma does not pile itself upon you, rather you yourself pile up karma over and over with your mind. When you can make the fetus take off its karma, and when you can eliminate its problems caused by karma and causality, your child won't be seriously ill and won't have the seeds of evil behavior or affinity with evil things. Therefore, even if you received a spirit with a lot of bad karma, you can still turn that around. Then the child will turn out well and will have affinity with good things. Although there is no intent on their part, the child naturally doesn't cause big problems or do bad things. When the child grows up into a good person, then this is being a dutiful son or daughter.

From the time you get pregnant, you need to begin educating your fetus. The first three months, the seventh month and the ninth month of the pregnancy are all very important stages for educating the fetus. Those stages are important because that is when what was input, according to how the fetus lived in the past, comes out in the present. Things continuously arise in the present according to how someone has lived in the past. These are what some people call fate and destiny. What are you going to do with those things that come out into this world because they were input? So people receive everything exactly as they did it, but they complain, saying, "What did I do wrong? Why do I suffer from these things?" Thus, in order to receive a child and get rid of those kinds of problems that the fetus may have, you have to educate the fetus.

While crying, many mothers have complained that their children skip school, sleep away from home, or run around with bad friends. So I said, "Do not yell at your children, or hit them. Because those things are caused by problems of mind, you have to cure them through mind. When your child comes home, without thinking, you say all kinds of things, such as 'What the hell is the matter with you! Do you want to be a ditch digger?! If you don't go to school, that's what will happen to you!' Because you treat your children with a harsh mind, your children behave exactly according to how you treated them. Because your mind and your child's mind are connected to each other, and because your mind and your child's mind are not two, you should raise the thought that 'Juingong, only you can brighten my child's mind,' and then release that thought there. Then, the light will be turned on instantly."

5. Handling Difficulties

Difficulties

Never see difficulties as being separate. Do not see them separately, such as "me" and "others," owner or guest. Don't be blinded by beautiful shapes, and don't be awed by great things. Because you exist, the world exists. Because you exist, all difficulties exist. Because all things in the universe are Hanmaum, all difficulties are certainly not different from you. Never be shaken. No matter whether it is Buddha, the King of Demons, or a Dharma-protecting spirit, everything is merely another shape of yourself.

Ultimately, all difficulties are not different from you. No matter how hard you try, you cannot avoid the numerous problems that confront you. When you let go and entrust with the belief that you and they are not two, then you are no longer afraid of any difficulties, and you can face them directly. After this, through those difficulties, you will be able to directly see the reality that nothing is created and nothing disappears.

If you try to find the substance of any difficulty, you will discover that it is empty. If you search for the substance of any defilement, it is empty. If you search for the substance of any greed, bad karma, or craving for love, they are all empty. They appear like a mirage or an illusion in inherently and completely empty space. They appear like white clouds or like a flash of lightning. People with certain eye diseases see flowers drifting in clear, empty space. All difficulties are like this, regardless of whether they are from inside or outside.

When you climb to the top of a high mountain and look at the houses below, you may feel that they are all about the same, without any clear distinction between big and small. Like this, try to apply this principle to your daily life. Then the differences between high and low, like and dislike, of all the things that confront you will begin to disappear. Further, try to meet all difficulties with a completely empty mind. Try to become like an empty boat. It moves as the wind blows and as the water flows. Because there is no "I" to raise up, there will be no colliding or suffering. Become a free person, like an empty boat.

Because you came out into this world, good things and bad things confront you. Thus there is no person or thing that you can resent. You must return everything as something that you have caused. Even though others bother you, you should return it as something that you have caused. Further, because your Juingong and others' Juingong are not two, you have to raise the thought that "Juingong, only you can solve it." Even though others may do bad things to you, you must know that you also behaved like that when you lacked wisdom. So, even though others bother you so much that you can't stand it, you should feel sorry because you have caused them to spend so much effort. You should also be thankful to them because they are causing your practice to mature. Otherwise, if you think that others will bother you, have bothered you, have deceived you, have hurt you, etc., then even though you try to raise mind to practice, it will be in vain. Therefore, you must go forward such that first, this practice starts with you; second, it again starts with you; and third, it again starts with you.

Whether or not you are going to be free from the

difficulties that confront you is a much more important issue than knowing whether or not they were caused by your karma. Therefore, know that all coming things are teachers that wake you up, so be thankful and let go completely. Regardless of what they are, and regardless of whether you have done them knowingly or unknowingly, they are the results that you have made. Thus know that there is no one you can blame or resent, so thoroughly let go and throw them away. When you do this, you can be free from them.

Bad circumstances are, in fact, another shape of Juingong, which is trying to teach you. Therefore, forgetting about your inherent mind because of circumstances is not acceptable and cannot be excused. In fact, when you understand, you realize that those things are Juingong caring for you. Thus you cannot avoid being thankful for the love from Juingong, which wants to teach you by doing even that. In fact, when difficulties come, you can obtain more in your practice. Thus, if difficulties come, take them as an opportunity to practice, and overcome them. It is more worthwhile when you overcome a mountain that is hard to cross.

Suffering

When problems occur, most people try to find solutions not from within themselves, but from someplace else. They rely on doctors and hospitals for problems with the physical body, and they try to solve their poverty by depending upon others' help. They ask about their own destiny from fortune tellers, and they rely upon schools for education. These kinds of things can be a temporary solution, but they cannot be the ultimate solution. It is said that clothes are wings,[46] but even though you wear very nice clothes, those clothes cannot become your body. Like this, although a solution seems good, if you find it anywhere other than inside yourself, then it is not a true solution. Thus it is said that you must find yourself. Everything is within you. You must find a hospital, doctor, cure, and solution from within yourself. If you wander around outside, you cannot bring out the infinite solutions that are inside. Paradise is not the place we find after going through many difficulties. Instead, we must practice such that paradise comes and finds us.

We are born according to karmic affinity. This itself is a product of cause and effect, so inherently it is suffering. This is because karma from previous lives accumulated, gathered together, and became the present being. However, if you think of this in a negative way, i.e., that it is the results of karma, then you will suffer endlessly. But if you change your thoughts and think of all of this as the process of practicing, then you cannot help saying "Thank you!" to your true self. Changing thoughts is like watering seedlings, and thinking of it as the results of karma and then suffering is like letting

---

46) This is a Korean expression meaning roughly that a nice appearance can create all kind of opportunities for you.

seedlings die of thirst. Thus, if you don't know, it is hell, and if you do know, it is paradise.

Diseases

If you sincerely believe in Juingong, then you do not need to ask Juingong to help you do something, or to make things go well. Juingong knows about the things that go well or poorly even better than you do, so you shouldn't say, "Please help me." Instead, just say, "Only Juingong can do it." This is not done with words, but with the meaning; it is raising One Thought through mind. Disease, poverty, and suffering all arise from mind. Hell also arises from your mind. Thus, if you have a disease, and you firmly return it, saying, "Only my Juingong can cure this disease," then all Bodhisattvas will instantly appear and help.

If you say, "Because it came out from that place, I'll return it to that place," then the lives of all cells, which gathered together because of cause and effect, will move throughout the body confidently and firmly, and will provide everything that is needed. Thus the disease will disappear. However, if you do not believe in Juingong, then even if something is wrong, those lives cannot function properly. This is like when a ship is in danger - if the crew does not know that there is an able captain, they will be full of confusion, running this way and that way.

Other people's Buddha-nature and your Buddha-nature are the same. Therefore, raising mind is based on sincerely believing in the principle of Hanmaum. For example, if your mother becomes seriously ill, firmly believe that "Juingong formed both me and my mother, and my mind and my mother's mind are Hanmaum. So if I raise my mind for my mother, then her illness will certainly be cured." Believing and entrusting like this is raising mind.

When your body is sick, if you say, "Juingong! Please cure it," then this is the same as praying. In this case, the one who prays and the one who receives the prayer are existing separately. Thus, it is said that you should watch and raise mind, saying, "Juingong! Because you do all things, take care of how this should happen." This is different from praying. This is like you talking to yourself with wordless words, with the heart that is heavy and sincere beyond description, and is beyond the mind of selfishness and egotistic thoughts. You speak from the mind that reflects things like a mirror reflects objects.

The medicine from mind is the best. If any part of the internal organs goes on strike, then a disease will occur. If the manager of your mind, Hanmaum, raises One Thought and releases it, saying, "Things that arise from that place have to be taken care of there," then it will be cured. When you do this, the disease may be cured at once, but sometimes it lasts a while longer. This is like Juingong assigning you homework in order to make you practice. Therefore, even though you feel a little better, you should not become complacent.

Dreams

Dreams are reality and reality is a dream. If you think that "dreams are dreams and reality is reality," then you cannot know the deeper place. Do not see dreams and reality as being separate. Even in a dream, you should not see things or difficulties as being separate from you, so that you do not become caught up in them. If you are aware that it is just a dream, then you will not chase after those things that happen there. Like this, those people who clearly know that defilements are a dream are never deceived by defilements.

Chapter 11

Religion and Daily Life

1. Bowing

True bowing means having the mind that humbles yourself and respects Buddhas, Bodhisattvas, and Seon masters. But at the same time, you should not become separate from Hanmaum, and should not lose your determination and resolution. Accordingly, even if you pray for the compassion of Buddhas and Bodhisattvas, you should put the center deep inside of yourself. Although you may be able to make some good fortune if your heart is extremely sincere, you cannot make infinite and true Virtue and Merit as long as you search outside of yourself.

When mind becomes one with Juingong, bowing to Buddha is practicing the path. When mind is separate from Juingong, bowing to Buddha becomes praying for good fortune; thus, there is no true Virtue and Merit. When mind becomes one with Juingong, respecting Buddha becomes respecting yourself. When mind is separate from Juingong, respecting Buddha becomes looking down on yourself.

When you return everything and bow once in front of Buddha, the present mind, past mind, and future mind all function as one mind. So bowing once can surpass bowing 10,000 times. When you bow and put your forehead on the ground in front of Buddha, it means that Buddha's mind and your mind are not two, and that Buddha's shape and your shape are not two. Thus your flesh bows to your Juingong.

In the beginning, when people are told to bow inwardly, they do not easily believe this. Thus, to a certain extent, it makes sense to raise up something outside. However, people of this advanced era have the ability to understand this. Thus you should keep holding inside and go forward. Further, in this very busy era, you have to run while thinking and you have to think while running. So if you have to do 108 bows or 3,000 bows, how can you practice? Because mind is beyond time and space, does not have form, and is completely free, what do you think if I say that bowing once is bowing 3,000 times? If you bow once extremely sincerely with Hanmaum, then it can exceed bowing even 30,000 times.

The Five Fragrances[47] are not some sort of material

incense. They are the beautiful fragrances that arise from inside of your mind. In every single thing you do, if there is no egotistic opinion in your intention, words, and actions, such that they do not become unworthy things, then this is the fragrance of precepts. Letting go inwardly to the foundation and going forward is the fragrance of meditation. You are naturally never caught and never attached; thus, you shine with the light of inherent nature. This is the fragrance of wisdom. Thus, as the middle way, without thoughts of throwing away or obtaining, you penetrate and hold up one fist. This is the fragrance of enlightenment. You and the whole together are bright, so there is nothing to be caught. This is the fragrance of ultimate enlightenment. When you have ceremonies in front of Buddha, studying mind is the Five Fragrances.

Bowing reverently to Buddha and Seon masters is bowing reverently to your true nature. Offering food to Buddhas and Seon masters is offering food to your Juingong. Indeed, the mind of Buddha, the mind of Bodhisattvas and Dharma protecting spirits, the mind of Patriarchs and Seon masters of the past, and the mind of all ancestors and all unenlightened beings are together inside of Hanmaum, your Juingong. Therefore, bowing reverently and offering food with Hanmaum is bowing reverently and offering food

---

47) These are the fragrance of precepts, of meditation, of wisdom, of liberation, and the fragrance of liberation together with all things. The recitation of the Five Fragrances is done during the evening ceremony at most temples in Korea.

together with all Buddhas and all unenlightened beings. Thus you must not forget your foundation, Juingong Hanmaum.

2. Studying Sutras

Those people who read sutras but miss the true meaning are like bees that hit the window and die while trying to get to the flowers on the other side.

The Buddha said, "If you have already crossed the river, throw away the raft." In this world, there are a lot of leftover rafts, i.e., the teachings of people who have already crossed the river. However, those rafts are not on this side of the river, they're on the other side of the river. Those rafts on the other side do not come to you even though you call them or motion at them to come over. Therefore, you have to make your own raft through your own efforts and cross the river. What is your own raft? It is your own true mind. Entrusting everything to your foundation and going forward is riding your raft and crossing the river.

When you feel free because your center of mind, your Jujangja, has arisen, you can read sutras such as the Heart Sutra, the Diamond Sutra, the Lotus Sutra, the Flower Ornament Sutra, etc. If you correctly brighten your mind and clearly see yourself, then you can refer to the teachings left by great teachers of the past. If you know your true self of the inner world, then when you read sutras you will be able to read them without separating the words and the blank paper. This is why it is said, "While reading sutras, do not read them. While not reading sutras, read them."

3. Keeping the Precepts

"Don't do this, don't do that" is not the true meaning of the precepts that the Buddha gave. Although something is extremely good, if you overdo it, then it can become bad. Although something is very bad, if you do it according to the needs and circumstances, then there is room for reconsideration. For example, the five precepts have usually been described as "do not...," but these days they can be read positively. For example, "Do not kill" becomes "Love all lives equally and compassionately." "Do not steal" becomes "Give alms, and make Virtue and Merit." "Do not engage in improper sexuality" becomes "Polish clear and clean actions with your body and mind." "Do not lie" becomes "Speak only truth and uphold trust." "Do not drink alcohol" becomes "Always have bright and upright wisdom." By understanding the precepts like this, the precepts are not something you keep by not doing. Rather, you keep them by putting Buddha's intention into action. If the fundamental mind is clear and upright, then there is nothing else that you need to uphold.

Once precepts are given, they are a burden. However, if you let go of all things to the foundation, then the precepts will be kept automatically, even though you do not constantly think about them. When this happens, precepts are the wings of freedom. Do not try to adapt yourself to the precepts. Rather, make the precepts that are already within you come out automatically.

Because you see yourself as only an unenlightened being, you don't trust yourself. As a result, you tie yourself up with the precepts. Rather than doing this, believe in the foundation of yourself, which is Buddha, and live freely. This is the positive way of keeping precepts that transcend the precepts. We, who are inherently Buddhas, live with our own light.

Those people who have escaped from the barrel will never be caught, regardless of what they do, because they can freely enter and leave the barrel. However, those people who haven't escaped from the barrel are often caught because they see, hear, act, and feel based upon the laws of the barrel. Thus, even though you are not caught, you should not do things that disturb other people's eyes and ears, such that they are caught by their own mind. Even though you can freely cross back and forth over the hills of the beyond, you should not provide any chances for other people to create bad karma. This is because all things rotate inclusively, not individually.

If you die, all precepts automatically drop away.

4. Teachers and the Place for Learning the Path

For a blind person, a cane is necessary, and for a person with a hurt leg, a crutch is necessary. Like this, for a practitioner, a teacher is necessary. When a blind person opens their eyes, they don't need a cane, because they have their own eyes. Like this, when true self appears, you don't need a separate teacher. However, until then, you must believe in and follow your teacher.

Taking refuge in the Sangha[48] does not mean that you should believe in sunims. The only thing you should believe in is your own Juingong. On the other hand, when you think that the actions, words, and intentions of a sunim all agree with each other, and do not deviate from common sense, then you can follow and accept that sunim as your teacher. In the process of practicing, you need not only an inner teacher, but also an outer teacher, who can help you with your experiences. Like this, for Won Hyo, there was Dae An,[49] and for Hui-ko, Bodhidharma was necessary.

Without using words, mountains silently tell us, "Live like a mountain." Water silently tells us, "Live like water."

48) Sangha traditionally refers to the ordained disciples of Buddha, but it sometimes means the entire community of Buddhist believers.

Flowers silently tell us, "Live like a flower." The root of a weed in harsh soil tells us, "Live wisely." All things tell us to live like them. Therefore, there is nothing that is not a teacher.

There is no place in the Buddha Realm that is not your place. Thus, no matter whether you are in the Dharma Hall or sitting on the toilet, because you exist at that place, true self exists together with you, and Buddha also exists together with you. Nevertheless, there are many people who ignore Juingong and wander around outside, trying to find a better place for praying or a better teacher. They don't know that they have their own Dharma Hall, and that the lights are always on and Buddha is always present inside of their Dharma Hall. A gardener is not someone who causes flowers to bloom on a dead tree.

---

49) Won Hyo (元曉), 617~686. Considered one of the greatest monks of Korea, He was an outstanding sunim who was known for the depth of his enlightenment and the commentaries that he wrote about various sutras, as well as his unconventional behavior. One famous story about him says that he spent a night in a cave, and being very thirsty during the night, found some water in a broken jar. In the morning, he saw that he had actually drunk from a broken skull and began to vomit. At the moment of vomiting, he realized enlightenment.

Dae An (大安), dates unknown. He was called "Dae An" (Great Peace) because he sometimes went through villages shouting "Dae An! Dae An!" He was a recluse, about whom almost nothing is known, other than that Won Hyo practiced under him after becoming enlightened.

5. True Offering and Giving

When all mind is combined, such that you think of everything as your body, as your own pain, as your own place, then how can your life be precious and others' life not be precious? This is the mind of a Bodhisattva and is true giving.

When you offer something, you must do it without doing. When you give, entrust it to Juingong and let go of it with extreme sincerity. Offering is like taking your money and buying something in a store. Thus, even though you donate, you are not giving it to others. Instead, you are receiving it for yourself.

Giving is compassion, and not giving can also be compassion; just make sure that it benefits others.

6. Reciting the Name of Buddha and Chanting Sutras

Bowing respectfully begins when you believe in Juingong. Only those people who do this can make the sounds of chanting sutras spread out all over the Buddha Realm. If you read sutras with such a mind, then Buddhas and Bodhisattvas will listen and it will widely and evenly spread out over every place. Because everything is non-dual, true Virtue and Merit are within the mind that reads sutras and recites mantras while seeing everything as not being separate. However, when I see the way some people practice, mantras are just mantras and reciting is only reciting. Without knowing the deep meaning, they just recite with only their mouth, with only their thoughts. Thus, their sincerity never reaches the Dharma Net in the unseen realm, and they are the only ones who hear it. When we recite the Heart Sutra, or the Thousand Hands Sutra, we also recite the visible and material laws and the invisible and non-material laws, which operate and live every moment. Therefore, by following those principles in our daily lives, we learn how to go and come without going and coming.

Some people think that they must recite Buddha's name everyday without fail. However, to those people in whom the thought of "I" does not arise, One Thought can become reciting Buddha's name, and One Thought can be automatically become using and the wheel of the Dharma. How can you ignore this principle and insist that it is correct to recite with only the mouth?

7. Believing in Outer Powers

If you are someone who blindly follows by praying towards the outside and lives while believing in only outer powers, then it can be said that you have lost the great and unlimited potential of a human being. You have also lost the capacity to become a Buddha, who is the Dharma-body. If you are a human being, then as the most advanced animal, you must know to reflect upon yourself.

If you discriminate between this place and that place, and if you distinguish between the name of this religion and that religion, then how can you experience the principle that everything is not two? If you are looking for this god or that god, then you will lose this god, that god, and even your own god.

8. Propagation

Only the person who deeply believes that they are the heir of Buddha and who is naturally filled with joy of the Dharma can make others enter the Buddha-dharma. Even though such a person does not open their mouth, and does not persuade with logic, they are already a true propagator of the Buddha-dharma.

9. Religious Conflicts

Religion is a name. It is the name that is made by people who live under the same roof, according to their circumstances and geographical location. Thus religion is not something to fight over. People fight because they want to fight. God does not tell them to fight, and Jesus does not tell them to fight. Buddha does not order them to fight, and Allah does not command them to fight. People just fight, but they try to say that they fight in the name of their supreme being.

10. Lighting Lamps in the Dharma Hall[50]

If you turn on a light with an extremely sincere heart, then that light is always on and combines as one with the universe and your mind. Therefore, do not say that you must light one of the small lamps in front of Buddha and that you must leave it lit for one hundred days. This is not lighting a lamp. In the middle of daily life, if you turn on the light of your mind, then the lamp will always be on. Thus people's mind is the lamp. If mind is bright, you will always be bright. However, just lighting an ordinary lamp does not make you bright.

Lighting a thousand candles in the Dharma Hall is not better than lighting the candle of mind once. If you turn on the light of mind, the entire universe will know it. But if you light a candle as only a candle, then only things near the candle will know it.

---

50) In many Buddhist countries, turning on small electric lamps or lighting candles in the Dharma Hall is done out of reverence and also sometimes done to make good fortune for that person or their family.

11. Chundo Jae: Ceremony to Lead the Dead to
   a Higher Realm

There are three levels to a Chundo Jae. At the first level, you do not know the principle of mind, and just recite and perform the ceremony according to instructions. At the next level, you know the principle of mind and entrust everything and raise mind for the dead, so it will be accomplished according to your ability to raise mind. The third level is when you know that, because the mind of all Buddhas and the mind of all ancestors are not two, all things are accomplished at and come out from and return to one place. Then regardless of whether you hold the ceremony or not, your ancestors are all led to a higher realm.

When you entrust everything and raise mind for the dead, the mind of all Buddhas and the mind of all ancestors, who worry about their children, combine together and become a huge brightness, that, in an instant, can lead the dead to a higher realm. When you know the principle of mind and can raise One Thought, then the minds of ancestors become one with your mind, so they are automatically led to a higher realm. Even though you do not light a candle, you have already lit a lamp with your mind, so everything will be accomplished inside of that lamp. When you hold a Chundo Jae, the Buddha who saves, the mind of the person who wants to help their ancestors, and the mind of the ancestors who receive the help are all together. However, if you don't believe this, then for your ancestors, higher realms become as far away as your lack of belief.

When an awakened person sees the spirit of the dead, they do not see a certain fixed shape. Instead, they see the level of mind that the dead person had while alive. Because the level of consciousness remains exactly the same after the body falls away, a Chundo Jae is leading them to a brighter level. This is like the blind being led by people who can see.

12. Jaesa: Memorial Service

In your daily life, earnestly tell everything to the inside of your mind. Then, because your parents, ancestors, all Bodhisattvas, and Dharma-protecting spirits exist inside of mind, your life itself becomes a memorial service for your parents and a ceremony for Buddha.

13. Releasing Lives[51]

When a fish flops around on the ground after a flood, putting the fish back into the water is truly releasing lives. If

---

51) In most Buddhist countries there are occasional ceremonies for "Releasing lives." At those times people usually release captive fish, turtles, and birds. However, in some places, selling captive animals is a thriving business, with people sometimes even waiting down-stream to recapture the animals that were released.

you catch fish that were living comfortably in the water, then you may kill them as you catch them or when you set them free. This is not releasing lives or compassionate behavior; it is committing a crime.

When a life does not have water, putting it back into water is releasing lives. When a family is evicted because they don't have money for the rent or to send their children to school,[52] putting them back into a home and giving them money for school is releasing lives.

14. Fate and Destiny

If mind is bright, then it is just bright, not because of fate. If mind is dark, then it is just dark, not because of destiny. In the Buddha's Dharma, there is no fate or destiny, and the three disasters and the eight hardships[53] also do not exist. The Buddha's Dharma is truly refreshing Dharma.

---

52) In Korea, the government pays for education only through junior high school. The costs for high school and above must be paid by the parents.

53) The three disasters are flood, fire, and wind. The eight hardships are hunger, thirst, cold, heat, water, fire, war, and disease.

Glossary

Bhikkuni

Female sunims who are fully ordained are called Bhikkuni(比丘尼) sunims, while male sunims who are fully ordained are called Bhikku(比丘) sunims. This can also be a polite way of indicating male or female sunims.

Buddha Realm(三千大千世界, Literally, "Three thousand, great thousand universe")

"Three" means the past, future and present. "Three" also means the Upper Realm, Middle Realm and Lower Realm. "Thousand" means combining them all together as one. When those are all combined together as one, it can be called "Great thousand universe." This one encompasses everything and functions non-dually. Because this is also what the word "Buddha" means, the "Three thousand, great thousand universe" can also be called the "Buddha Realm."

cultivating mind

This includes learning how mind works, applying that knowledge, experimenting with it, and gaining experiences in order to become a free person. Studying mind, polishing mind, and cultivating mind are all similar expressions.

Defilements(煩惱, klesa)

Defilements refer to all the properties that dull the mind and are the basis for all unwholesome actions and things that bind people to the cycle of birth and death.

Dharma-body(法身, dharmakaya)

If One Thought arises, then it is the Dharma-body. "If it just remains quietly, it's Buddha. If a thought arises, it's the Dharma-body, and if it moves, it's the Transformation-body."

Dharma-realm(法界, dharmadhatu)

This includes all of the material and non-material realms combined together, and also the fundamental order and principles according to which the material and non-material realms function.

emptiness (空, sunyata)

This does not mean that there is nothing; rather, it means that everything changes and manifests every instant, without remaining stationary. It is called emptiness because everything constantly changes and manifests, without any permanent, fixed shape, and is too diverse to be described.

empty space(虛空)

The space between the things we can see. It is the space that we usually think of as having nothing in it but air. This term usually doesn't refer to outer space.

Five Fragrances

These are the fragrance of precepts, of meditation, of wisdom, of liberation, and the fragrance of liberation together with all things. The recitation of the Five Fragrances is done during the evening ceremony at most temples in Korea.

Five subtle powers

The five subtle powers are the ability to hear anything at any place, the ability to see anything at any place, the ability to know others' thoughts and feelings, the ability to know past, present, and future lives, and the ability to appear anywhere, without moving your body.

Four types of lives

The four types of lives are lives born from eggs, born from the womb, born from moisture, and born through transformation.

good fortune (福德, 祈福)

Material or spiritual benefits that last for only a limited amount of time.

great saving power

This is the ability to solve problems and take care of things by raising One Thought.

Hanmaum (한마음, [han-ma-um])

"Han" means one, great, and combined, while "maum" means mind, as well as heart, and also means the universal consciousness that is the same in every thing and every place. Thus, "Hanmaum" means the one, great, combined mind and the inter-connectedness of everything and the wholeness that includes everything.

haengja (行者, 〔haeng-ja〕)

This is someone who has entered a temple and wants to become a sunim, but who has yet to take formal vows. This is considered a training period usually lasting between one and three years, where the haengja can see if they really want to become a sunim, and it also gives the temple a chance to evaluate the haengja.

hwadu (話頭, Chin.-hua-tou, Jap.-koan)

Traditionally, the key phrase of an episode from the life of an ancient master(kung-an) and was used for awakening practitioners, and could not be understood intellectually. This developed into a formal training system using several hundred of the traditional 1,700 kung-ans. But hwadus are also fundamental questions arising from inside that we have to resolve. It has been said that your life itself is the fundamental hwadu that you must first solve.

Jujangja (拄杖者, 〔ju-jang-ja〕)

This usually refers to the staff carried by Buddhist monks, but it also can mean a person's center of mind.

Juingong(主人空, 〔ju-in-gong〕)

"Juin" means the true owner, the true doer, and "gong" means completely empty, so "Juingong" means the owner, the doer that is empty, that is without any fixed shape, and which always changes and manifests.

kalpa (劫)

An immensely long period of time. Traditionally described as the time it would take to wear away a rock that formed a cube ten miles high, wide, and long, if a piece of silk brushed against it once every hundred years.

karmic affinity (인연, 因緣)

This is similar to karma, but it refers to the specific connection or attraction between people or things, due to previous karmic relationships.

Kun Sunim(큰스님)

The polite way of addressing a very senior sunim, but it also can refer to a sunim considered awakened or outstanding in some other aspect of practice or study.

Lower Realm

see Three Realms

Middle Realm

see Three Realms

mind (마음, 心)

Mind, in this text, does not refer to the brain or intellect. Mind has been described as the foundation of everything, and is intangible, invisible, beyond space and time, and has no beginning or end. In Asia, if you ask someone where their mind is, they will point to their chest. It is the character for mind that has been translated as "Heart" in the "Heart Sutra."

One Thought (한생각)

This means raising a thought from the foundation, as opposed to the discriminating intellect. One Thought from the foundation will cause all lives in your body to move according to that thought.

Realm of Good Beings(善神世界)

This is traditionally thought of as beings of the Upper Realm who devote their energies to helping human beings and other beings in the Middle and Lower Realms. Dae Haeng Kun Sunim explains this as the workings and manifestation of your mind through the invisible realms.

Samadhi(三昧)

Samadhi has been defined many ways, but it is often described as a non-dualistic state of consciousness in which subject and object become one.

Samini(沙彌尼, **sramaneri**)

This is the first level of ordination for a sunim. Women

are called Samini(沙彌尼, sramaneri) sunims, and men are called Sami(沙彌, sramanera) sunims. Full ordination usually takes place after at least four more years.

samsara (輪廻)

This is the idea that all living things repeatedly pass through life and death. Like a continually spinning wheel, sentient beings are continuously reborn and dying. In Buddhism, one is said to continually pass through the three realms(desire, form, and formless) and the six types of existence(god, demi-god, human, animal, hungry ghost, and hell-being).

Sangha

Sangha traditionally refers to the ordained disciples of Buddha, but it sometimes means the entire community of Buddhist believers.

Seon (禪, dhyana, ch'an, zen)

Seon means that your mind is undisturbed while you let go of everything and know that all visible and invisible things come out from and return to Juingong.

Shimsung (심성, 心性)

When mind is raised such that the material and non-material realms combine together and energy and ability come out from them it is called "Shimsung."

sunim (스님)

The Korean word for a Buddhist monk or nun. Also the polite way of addressing a Korean monk or nun. For example, addressing them by their Dharma name and then Sunim, or sometimes just Sunim. See Kun Sunim.

Three Realms (三界, trilokadhatu)

The Upper Realm, which is the realm of more advanced beings, the Middle Realm, which is the realm of human beings and the Lower Realm, which is the realm of less developed beings and the hell realms.

Three Times (三世)

The past, present, and future.

Transformation-body (化身, nirmanakaya)

When a Dharma-body changes into manifestation-bodies.

"If it just remains quietly, it's Buddha. If a thought arises, it's the Dharma-body, and if it moves, it's the Transformation body."

Tushita Heaven (都率天)

A heavenly realm that is the last stopping place of a Buddha before his decent and rebirth on Earth. At present, the abode of the future Buddha, Maitreya.

Upper Realm

see Three Realms

Virtue and Merit(功德)

Helping people or beings unconditionally and non-dually, without any thought of self or other. It becomes Virtue and Merit when you "do without doing," that is, doing something without the thought that "I did..." Because it is done unconditionally, all beings benefit from it.

Watching(觀)

The Korean word that has been translated here as "watching" can also mean observing, being aware, and mindfulness.

HanMaUm Seon Center

Anyang-city, Korea

Overseas HanMaUm Seon Centers

CENTRAL

HanMaUm Seon Center
101-62, Seoksu-dong, Manan-gu,
Anyang-city, Kyonggi-do, 430-040
KOREA
TEL : 0343-470-3100
FAX : 0343-470-3116
http://www.hanmaum.org/

If you need more information about
Dae Haeng Sunim's teachings,
please contact us.

Hanmaum Translation Group
101-62, Seoksu-dong, Manan-gu,
Anyang-city, Kyonggi-do, 430-040
KOREA
TEL : 82-343-471-6926/6927
FAX : 82-343-471-6928

NEW YORK
144-39, 32 Ave. Flushing, NY 11354
TEL : 718-460-2019, FAX : 718-939-3974

WASHINGTON D.C.
7807 Trammell Rd. Annandale, VA 22003
TEL : 703-560-5166, FAX : 703-560-5166

LOS ANGELES
210 N. Catalina St. LA, CA 90004
TEL : 213-382-1711, FAX : 213-386-8852

CHICAGO
7852 N. Lincoln Ave. Skokie, IL 60077
TEL : 847-674-0811, FAX : 847-674-2280

BUENOS AIRES
Miro 1575, CP1406, Rep. Argentina
TEL : 54-11-4921-9286
FAX : 54-11-4921-9286

TUCUMAN
Av. Aconqiza 5250, El Corte,
Yerba Buena, CP4107
Tucuman, Rep. Argentina
TEL : 54-381-425-1400
FAX : 54-381-425-1400

CANADA
20 Mobile Dr. North York, Ontario
M4A 1H9 Canada
TEL : 416-750-7943, FAX : 416-750-3090

GERMANY
Broicherdorf Str. 102, 41564 Kaarst,
Germany
TEL : 49-2131-969551
FAX : 49-2131-969552

THAILAND
43 soi Pattanavet Sukhumvit 71
Bangkok, Thailand
TEL: 662-711-2005, FAX: 662-391-6425